THE SALISBURY HOARD

I.M. Stead

TEMPUS

First published 1998

Published by:
Tempus Publishing Limited
The Mill, Brimscombe Port
Stroud, Gloucestershire, GL5 2QG

Typesetting and origination by Tempus Publishing Ltd.
Printed and bound in Great Britain

British Library Cataloguing in Publication Data.
A catalogue record for this book is available from the British Library

ISBN 07524 1404 6

Contents

List of colour plates   4

List of text figures   5

Dramatis Personae   6

Foreword by Colin Renfrew
(Lord Renfrew of Kaimsthorn)   7

Preface   11

PART I : THE SALISBURY HOARD

1   The Miniature Shields   13
2   John of Salisbury   27
3   The Arrests   47
4   The Excavation   57
5   The Collections   73
6   The Trial   85
7   The Acquisition   101
8   The Archaeology   109

PART II : THE DISCOVERY AND PROTECTION
           OF ANTIQUITIES

9   Provenance   125
10   Context   139
11   Protection   149

Index   155

The illustrations

Colour Plates (between pages 64 and 65)

1   Decorated bronze miniature shield
2   Bronze socketed axes from the Salisbury Hoard
3   Bronze socketed axes, spearheads, daggers and gouges from
       the Salisbury Hoard
4   Bronze chisels, miniature cauldrons and other artefacts from
       the Salisbury Hoard
5   Bronze artefacts from the Salisbury Hoard
6   Bronze artefacts from the 'Gloucestershire' Hoard
7   Two joining fragments of a bronze miniature shield
8   The Red Lion, Salisbury
9   Photographs, artefacts and packaging seized when Garriock
       was arrested
10   The re-discovery of the site of the Salisbury Hoard in 1994
11   The Drott stripping top-soil at Netherhampton
12   The pit revealed in plan, before excavation
13   The pit in course of excavation
14   Hoard B
15   Joining fragments of bronze
16   Razors and other bronze artefacts from the Salisbury Hoard
17   Stages in the evolution of the bronze axe
18   Part of the Hounslow Hoard
19   The two terminals of a gold torque from Bawsey
20   Bronze artefact from Daneswick
21   Roman bronze box with enamel ornament, from Elsenham
22   Snettisham: selection of artefacts
23   Snettisham: hoard of gold torques

Cover illustrations
The front cover shows the re-discovery of the site of the Salisbury
Hoard; the back cover the photographs and artefacts seized on
Garriock's arrest

Text Figures

1	Two decorated bronze miniature shields	15
2	Bronze bindings from Iron Age shields, with a distribution map	19
3	Plotting of the magnetometer survey	62
4	Plan of the trenches excavated	63
5	Section through the pit	68
6	A chart illustrating the distribution routes of some of the artefacts from the Salisbury Hoard	74
7	Record drawings of two bronze razors	105
8	Classification of artefacts from the Salisbury Hoard	108
9	Miniature bronze cauldrons	116
10	Classification of artefacts from the 'Batheaston' Hoard	121
11	Bronze brooches, said to be from Wallingford	128
12	Bronze helmet from the Watney Collection	130
13	The decorated back of a bronze mirror from Chilham Castle	142

Dramatis Personae

Some of the characters who are mentioned more than once in the story of the Salisbury Hoard

Antiquities collectors
Peter Day, Diss, Norfolk
John Fowler, Exmouth, Devon
Barbara Goldstein, Salt Lake City, USA
Jonathan Rosen, USA
Mr Smith, Scottish farmer
Antiquities Dealers
Rose Anderson, Lord McAlpine's
    assistant
Maurice Braham, an associate of
    Lord McAlpine
Peter Clayton, Seaby's, Davies St,
    London W1
John Cummings, Grantham, Lincs
Susan Hadida, Secretary of the
    Antiquities Dealers Association
Malcolm Hay
Lord McAlpine, Cork Street,
    London W1
C. J. Martin, Southgate, London N14
David Miller, Hemel Hempstead,
    Herts
Nigel Mills, South Woodford,
    London E18
John Mussel, editor of
    Coin and Medal News
Julia Schottlander
Robin Symes, Ormond Yard,
    London W1
Bill Veres
Nicholas Wright, London NW6
Archaeologists
Clare Conybeare, freelance,
    formerly Salisbury Museum
Mark Corney, Royal Commission on
    Historical Monuments
    (England), Salisbury
Nick Griffiths, freelance illustrator
Andrew Lawson, Director,
    Wessex Archaeology
Peter Northover, Department of
    Metallurgy, Oxford University
Bemerton Farm, Netherhampton
Mr Bright, farm manager
Reginal Cook, farmer
Pamela Lowrie, Cook's daughter
Mr Oglethorpe, solicitor

British Museum
Robert Anderson, Director
    (from 1992)
Andrew Burnett, Keeper of
    Coins and Medals
Fran Dunkels, Press Office
George Morris, Secretary
Sir David Wilson, Director (to 1992)
*Department of Prehistoric and Romano-
British Antiquities, British Museum*:
Ian Longworth, Keeper (to 1995)
Stuart Needham,
    Bronze Age antiquities
Tim Potter, Keeper (from 1995)
Ian Stead, Iron Age antiquities
Excavation team
Ian Blomeley, freelance archaeologist
Peter Makey, freelance archaeologist
Tony Pacitto, freelance archaeologist
Tony Spence, Senior Museum
    Assistant, British Museum
Sheelagh Stead, wife of the writer and
    freelance archaeologist
Dave Webb, Senior Photographer,
    British Museum
Journalist
David Keys, *The Independent*
Legal
Richard Atkins, Crown Prosecution
    Service
Jonathan Laidler, prosecuting barrister
Miss Smith, Cummings' barrister
Metal detectorists
Brian Cavill, photographer, Swindon
James Garriock ('John'), Salisbury
Terry Rossiter, Salisbury
Museum curators
Paul Robinson, Devizes Museum
Peter Saunders, Salisbury Museum
Alison Sheridan, National Museums of
    Scotland
Andrew Sherratt, Ashmolean Museum
Police
Metropolitan Police, Holborn
DS Pete Basnett
DC Andy Cockburn
DS Rick Player
DCI Jack Woods
Art and Antiques Squad
DS Tony Russell

Foreword

by Colin Renfrew
(Lord Renfrew of Kaimsthorn)

This remarkable book is in the first place an archaeological 'Whodunnit' of the first class. The story begins promisingly with the sale to the British Museum from what one would have thought an impeccable source — a peer of the realm, once a high officer in the Conservative Party — of some rather strange and hitherto unrecorded antiquities, a series of 22 bronze miniature shields from the British Iron Age, of such evident rarity that a price of £55,000 was agreed. But soon it became apparent that these curious items were part of a much larger hoard, a spectacular find of prehistoric metalwork, which came to be called 'the Salisbury Hoard'. The author, who was at the time the principal specialist on the Iron Age in the relevant Department of the British Museum, set himself the task of investigating the circumstances of the find, and of tracing the remainder of the loot. For loot it was. It soon became clear that the hoard might have been discovered by 'nighthawks', members of that clandestine fraternity of illicit metal-detectorists who go secretly and often illegally by night onto private land in search of marketable antiquities. These they conceal, and sell in secret to dealers of questionable honesty, who do not enquire too deeply into the source of the by-now 'unprovenanced' antiquities. They in turn sell the antiquities on to dealers of better public repute, but who somehow on occasion likewise avoid asking too many awkward questions about the find circumstances, and are content to sell them as 'unprovenanced'.

Ian Stead set himself the objective of unravelling this chain of sometimes murky contacts, and of tracing the Hoard back to its original findspot. The story took him through the premises of reputable dealers, to secret meetings with 'John of Salisbury' in The Red Lion in that city, and to the arrest and trial of the metal-detectorists and dealer involved, to the conviction of some of them, and to the location and re-excavation of the original findspot.

Yet this book is something more than a straightforward piece of sleuthing. In laying bare the facts about the Salisbury Hoard, the author takes the lid off what is now an extensive trade in this country in illicit antiquities. And he makes clear that the main objections to this trade are not simply the economic questions of ownership, sale and profit. The real loss to archaeology and to our heritage is the loss of information which takes place when finds are split up and removed in secret from their findspot. It should be said at once that many metal-detectorists behave perfectly reputably. They ensure that they have the agreement of the landowner before prospecting , and take great care to show their finds to museum specialists who can arrange that they are noted by the new National Recording Scheme for Archaeological Objects. But when this is not done, the real value of the find — as a source of information about the past — is irretrievably lost. The story told here reveals more clearly than ever before the extent to which our national heritage is being systematically looted, plundered for personal gain, and the degree to which antiquities dealers and private collectors, by handling objects without known provenance, may contribute, wittingly or unwittingly, to this process. It is, after all, their money which goes ultimately to reward the looters and the shady dealers who buy directly and secretly from them.

Ironically, if the finds had been made of silver or of gold, they would have been protected under the law on Treasure (formerly known as 'Treasure Trove'). But at present only finds of gold and silver are protected in this way. Sadly England has no adequate antiquities legislation — hence the need for the new voluntary recording scheme.

And what about museums — should they be fuelling this process by paying good money for illicit antiquities? In general the answer must be no: museums should not buy antiquities without known provenance which may, in all likelihood, derive from clandestine excavations. Indeed the British Museum now has a policy which, in line with that of the Museums Association, prevents it from doing so, or even from accepting such unprovenanced finds as a gift (as I, as a Trustee of the British Museum should be well aware). But it is increasingly recognised that a national museum has some responsibility to act as a repository for any important antiquities found within its national boundaries, just as do regional museums in relation to finds from their region, even when the precise find circumstances have been lost. At the same time, no museum should make a purchase which conspicuously rewards looters and thereby fuels the looting process. By paying the well-respected London dealer Lord McAlpine the significant sum of £55,000 for the bronze shields, even though he himself could reasonably say that he bought them in good faith, the British Museum might be open to criticism. For it can certainly be argued that the payment of so large a sum for unprovenanced antiquities sends a signal to looters that their night-time work is likely to be well rewarded.

So in retrospect I think that the Museum may have been wrong to purchase them for so large a sum in the first place. And it certainly lost out as a result. For when it emerged that the original owner of the land where the finds were made (and hence their rightful owner) had been deprived of her property , the British Museum felt obliged to hand them back to her without waiting for any formal legal claims. But when it then turned to Lord McAlpine to ask for its money back, no encouraging reply was received, and certainly no money. The finds are however of such importance that the British Museum subsequently encouraged the owner herself to sell them (or, as it turned out, to make them available in lieu of Inheritance Tax), which means that the British Museum on behalf of the nation has had in effect to buy them twice over: once from Lord McAlpine and then once again from the rightful owner, i.e. the landowner, after first handing them back to her.

And was it worth all the fuss? Were the miniature bronze shields worth all the effort which Ian Stead and his colleagues have expended in tracking down their original source and, as he describes in this book, tracing most of the hundreds of other looted objects which were found in association with them by the metal-detectorists in their clandestine dig at Netherhampton? The answer is an emphatic 'yes'. For this was no ordinary find, not just another small hoard of bronze objects originally buried during the pre-Roman Iron Age around 100 BC. For as Ian Stead has definitively documented, these Iron Age shields were part of a very much larger deposit of more than 500 objects which includes a series of bronze objects of much earlier date, going back to bronze and even copper flat axes which had been made more than two thousand years earlier, perhaps around 2400 BC. The range of objects makes clear that this was a very special deposit, perhaps from a shrine or sanctuary, and certainly not just a job lot of scrap metal kept in reserve for the next visit by the itinerant metal smith. But the exciting thing is that we do not otherwise *know* of such sanctuaries in Britain, where objects already two thousand years old would be kept and respected, and ultimately buried with other more recent offerings. The find has important implications for our understanding of how our Iron Age ancestors themselves conceived of the notion of time and the idea of antiquity. For the surprising outcome is that the people who buried the Salisbury Hoard were in a sense themselves antiquarians, with a high degree of respect and veneration for the past — certainly a good deal more than the looters who made the discovery and sold it piecemeal.

The project of sleuthing becomes, along the way in itself a significant act of recovering our lost past, indeed our looted past. For in restoring the original context of the Salisbury Hoard, Ian Stead has been able to write a whole otherwise unrecorded chapter of British prehistory. In it he can document that our Iron Age ancestors kept and presumably venerated antiquities which had themselves been in existence for a longer period, when the Hoard came to be buried, than the period of time which has elapsed since that burial up to our own day. That is a new revelation about the past of Britain. It is almost humbling to think that our Iron Age predecessors shortly before the Roman conquest were already respecting their own past and the antiquities from their own prehistory. This new perspective about the respect for time and for the objects of antiquity in the intellectual climate of two thousand years ago becomes itself an important part of our knowledge and understanding of the past of Britain, and hence of our own heritage.

This book thus may begin as a thriller, and a rather unusual one at that. It becomes a clear demonstration and documentation of how much we lose when antiquities are divorced from their context by looting, and of how much we still stand to learn about the past when finders act responsibly, and when dealers and collectors decline to connive in the looting process by buying unprovenanced antiquities. And it ends with this extraordinary and unexpected new glimpse of the veneration with which our ancestors treated their own early past.

Preface

The story of the Salisbury Hoard has to be told in detail in order to convince archaeologists that this incredible collection really was buried on one occasion in antiquity. It also serves to illustrate the vulnerability of antiquities in England to the whims of the finders and dealers.

Collectors, metal detectorists, dealers and auction houses are all concerned with antiquities, but their attitudes and values differ from those of archaeologists. Sometimes the different approaches lead to misunderstanding and even outright animosity. The story of the discovery and recovery of the Salisbury Hoard illustrates these problems and may help all parties to have a better understanding of them.

The information was gathered while I worked at the British Museum, in charge of Iron Age antiquities in the Department of Prehistoric and Romano-British Antiquities. Several colleagues in the Museum helped in my investigation of the Salisbury Hoard, and two of them in particular played important roles. Ian Longworth gave me free rein to pursue my researches, as always, and was a constant source of encouragement and wise advice. Stuart Needham took an active part in the work, advised me on matters pertaining to Bronze Age antiquities, and criticised the present text. He is a tough critic, and his encouragement is greatly appreciated. Of course I am responsible for all the views expressed in this text, which do not necessarily reflect the opinions of either my colleagues or the Trustees of the British Museum.

The people who combined to bring this story to light feature in the text, and I am grateful to all those who helped me. Several deserve special thanks: of the archaeologists, Clare Conybeare, who was an invaluable source of both information and support; from the collector/dealer fraternity, Peter Day, who was the first to appreciate the full significance of the find, and Peter Clayton, who made tremendous efforts to bring the matter to a satisfactory conclusion for all concerned; and the police investigation would never have got underway but for DCI Jack Woods, an impressive detective with a real interest in the past. During the investigation some information was received in confidence, but in due course everything came into the open, so confidential material is related in its correct chronological position in the story.

Brian Cavill generously gave me permission to publish his unique photographs of the hoard, and the other photographs are reproduced by courtesy of the Trustees of the British Museum. Dave Webb took the photographs in the field, and most of the studio photographs are by Sandra Marshall. The line-drawings were coordinated by Karen Hughes, and their sources are acknowledged in the captions.

PART I THE SALISBURY HOARD

1. The Miniature Shields

My involvement with the Salisbury Hoard started in July 1988. One of my colleagues had established a contact with a London dealer, Lord McAlpine, and occasionally visited his rooms at Cork Street where some good-quality antiquities were on offer. Alistair McAlpine is a member of the family that owns one of the big construction companies, but is better known as a most successful Treasurer of the Conservative Party and a confidant of Lady Thatcher. On one visit my colleague had noticed a very fine decorated Iron Age linch-pin, so he suggested that I should go along with him to see it.

The linch-pin proved every bit as good as he had indicated. At that time McAlpine was on the second floor at 33 Cork Street in dark cluttered rooms that seemed to belong to another century. A padded door with spy-hole opened onto a long corridor with a large room at the end, and a smaller room at the side overlooking the street. McAlpine was in the smaller room, with a couple of arm-chairs by a fireplace, the door facing the window and a central table. An enormous fixture filled the wall opposite the fireplace, with four or five stacks of drawers in its lower part and bookshelves above. The drawers were full of antiquities and there were others, including Anglo-Saxon pots, in front of the books. We had coffee while we chatted and examined the drawers, and McAlpine stayed with us the whole time. I was surprised at the quality of the antiquities, and apart from the linch-pin I was particularly impressed by four decorated terrets (rein-rings) and a couple of vessel-mounts. McAlpine was very happy to lend them, with a view to either recording or purchase. All were inscribed with M numbers, which were listed in a Register; each entry was checked by Rose Anderson, McAlpine's assistant, but none had a recorded provenance.

One other item that caught my eye was a miniature shield. Cut from sheet bronze and only 60mm (2¼in) long, it was modelled on a full-size military shield and would have been used as a votive offering at a temple. It was unprovenanced, and could have come from anywhere because the collection was not confined to British pieces; the decorated linch-pin, for instance, was almost certainly continental. McAlpine asked if I was particularly interested in miniature shields: I said that they were quite rare in Britain, about a dozen of them, not many to get interested in. So he told me about a collection of miniature shields, some of them decorated, that had recently come on the market. Would I like to see them if he could bring them together? I had never heard of decorated miniature shields, so certainly I wanted to see them.

Back at the Museum, we realised that one of the vessel-mounts just borrowed from McAlpine had in fact been stolen from the Ryedale Folk Museum, in North Yorkshire. It had surfaced before, submitted to the British Museum by a collector/dealer called Nicholas Wright, and we had informed the police at Malton but apparently no action had been taken. I telephoned McAlpine and passed on the bad news. He was shocked and said that he would get in touch with the owner. He also said that he had managed to borrow the miniature shields; would I like to see them? I went round that day, taking papers showing that the vessel-mount was ex-Hildyard Collection, on loan to the Ryedale Folk Museum, Hutton-le-Hole. McAlpine had the shields spread across the table in the middle of his room, and they were fantastic. Twenty-two of them, including four with decoration, one quite magnificent. Two were oval but the rest were 'hide-shaped', with convex sides and concave ends, a form at that time unknown **(Fig 1, Colour plate 1)**. Some were broken and several had been carefully repaired; one had been repaired in antiquity. McAlpine said that they had come to him from two or three different sources, but ultimately they were all from the same find. He thought that they might be from the West Country, perhaps Gloucestershire, but he seemed to have little interest in provenance. I said that the Museum would certainly like to acquire them, so he promised to get them together and offer them to us.

The next problem was raising the money, because a substantial sum was needed. The Director (then Sir David Wilson), typically, was enthusiastic and decided to purchase the one continental item (the linch-pin) on its own and lump the British pieces together for separate consideration. So the miniature shields were grouped with the four decorated terrets and the one remaining vessel-mount, a lot

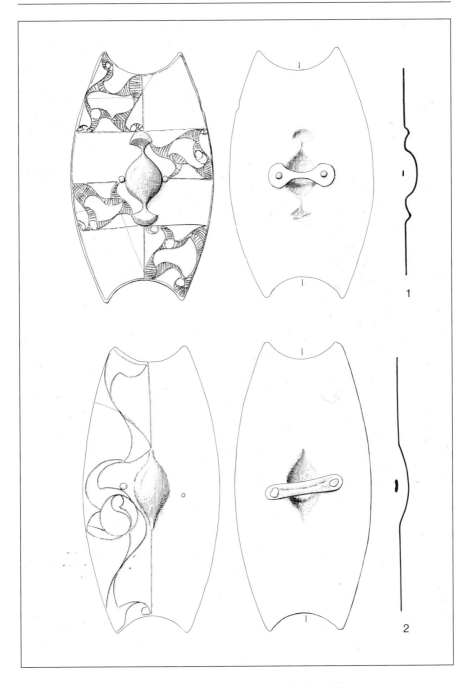

1   Two of the decorated bronze miniature shields (full size).
Drawn by Stephen Crummy.

for which McAlpine wanted £80,000. As the Purchase Grant was at a low ebb, it being late in the financial year, the National Heritage Memorial Fund was approached. Oliver Harris, the Director of the Fund, was worried by the absence of a provenance for any of the items, but was assured that the British Museum Trustees had considered this aspect very carefully. The Trustees had concluded that the items were certainly British, important and unusual: the overriding issue was to preserve them together in this country rather than to have them dispersed and perhaps sent abroad. The Fund was not entirely convinced, and although it offered up to £60,000 towards the purchase a condition was made that an indemnity be obtained from Lord McAlpine, so that should his title prove faulty he would refund the purchase price to the British Museum with interest. Our Trustees, however, felt that this approach was impracticable and offered instead that the British Museum would reimburse the Fund if their title was successfully challenged. This was accepted.

The purchase of these antiquities prompted the Trustees to adopt a formal policy concerning the acquisition of British items not found during an excavation, and the relevant statement was quoted in full in David Wilson's book, *The British Museum: Purpose and Politics* (1989), pp 33–4: 'The British Museum deplores the deliberate removal of ancient artefacts from British soil other than by properly directed archaeological excavation, especially when the context of those artefacts is thereby left unrecorded and severely damaged. However, although the unauthorised excavation of such material from a scheduled monument is illegal and can never be condoned, much of what is discovered elsewhere is brought to light lawfully; persons in possession of it often have a legal title to dispose of it as they think fit. In these circumstances, the Museum has an overriding duty to try to acquire such finds as it considers to be appropriate to the national collection. To refuse to follow this course would entail a serious loss to our heritage, since we would then lose the chance to see and record a great many objects. The Museum understands, and shares, the concern of the archaeological world, but since there is a ready market both here and abroad, the situation will not be remedied by a museum embargo. Selective acquisition remains, in our view, not only the practical, but also the proper course.'

The acquisition of the miniature shields was not the end of the matter. The collection was so important that we had to make a determined effort to recover their provenance. McAlpine had given one direct clue, perhaps West Country, possibly Gloucestershire, but he had also said that he had obtained the shields from two or three different sources. Dealers never reveal details of their transactions so I could get no more information directly, but the fact that two or three different sources were involved suggested that quite a few people might know about them, so we started making enquiries. Following the Gloucestershire lead, we contacted David Viner (Cirencester Museum) but the only miniature shield he had heard of recently was one with the Oxford Archaeological Unit. Paul Robinson (Devizes Museum), who had many contacts in the metal detecting world, provided some useful information. He had heard that there were miniature shields, including some with 'Early La Tène ornament', in a hoard of predominantly Late Bronze Age artefacts found by metal detectorists somewhere in south Wiltshire. He thought that the Ashmolean Museum might have more details. I also spoke to Peter Clayton who looked after antiquities for Seaby's, the London dealers. Peter was in a unique position, straddling the line between the dealing world and professional archaeology: he used to work for the British Museum, on the publication side, still lectures widely on Egyptology, and maintained a close contact with us. He, too, had heard rumours of miniature shields, perhaps 10 or 12 of them, in a hoard of Bronze Age bronzes known as the Salisbury Hoard. The miniature shields dated no earlier than, say, 200 BC, and a hoard of Bronze Age antiquities would be at least 500 years earlier. It seemed most unlikely that the two would have been found together. But despite the anachronism Peter assured me that the word in the trade was that the shields had definitely been found with Late Bronze Age artefacts. Two antiquities dealers, David Miller and Maurice Braham, had either seen or handled them. Stuart Needham, who curates the Bronze Age antiquities at the British Museum, had also heard of the Salisbury Hoard. It was supposed to be enormous, and some rumours gave its provenance as Dorchester, Dorset: perhaps one or two different discoveries had been conflated. Stuart knew nothing about miniature shields, but he had heard that the hoard included a pile of small bronze bowls — and they did not sound like Late Bronze Age artefacts.

I had had previous contacts with David Miller, one of the dealers mentioned, so I wrote to him, but his reponse was negative: he had 'not encountered even a rumour' of the miniature shields. He was aware of a number of axes in the trade about three years previously (ie about 1986) though he had no knowledge of their provenance. Andrew Sherratt, at the Ashmolean Museum, had heard of the Salisbury Hoard but had not seen any of it. He too had been intrigued by a reference to Iron Age miniature shields amongst the

Bronze Age antiquities, but his informant, a dealer from Stroud, Brian Carter, had not provided a detailed description. I spoke about the problem to Nigel Mills, who has a stall at the Covent Garden market, and he suggested that information might be forthcoming if he were to publish a photograph in one of the metal detecting journals. So we photographed two of them together — one of the distinctive hide-shaped shields from the Salisbury Hoard and a more normal oval shield. But Nigel did not take it further.

Another clue was provided by the shields themselves. Several had been repaired, one in antiquity, but most in relatively recent times. The repairs had been secured by strips of copper, on the back, and one had become detached. In the Conservation workshop it was examined by Simon Dove and Ian McIntyre who thought that the strip had been attached by Durafix or some related glue, which suggested that it had not been done before the 1940s. It was competent work, but it puzzled them: Victorians would have used solder, and anyone with a modern training would have used fibre-glass.

There the matter rested for over a year, until I revived it in July 1990 when I was completing a paper on Iron Age shields for the *Antiquaries Journal*. I had been studying the miniature shields and had realised that their curious hide-shape explained an artefact that had puzzled archaeologists for years. The mystery object was a short length of bronze binding, roughly V-shaped with a knob at the point of the 'V'. When a sufficient length survived one arm of the 'V' was straight and the other curved **(Fig 2)**. There were several of these distinctive pieces in our museums, and those with a context belonged to the Iron Age. In the past they had been identified as scabbard bindings, but that did not explain the curved arm. Having seen the miniatures the explanation was obvious: they were the bronze bindings of the corners of full-size hide-shaped shields that would otherwise have been made of wood and leather. Such shields must have been relatively common in the British Iron Age. I had prepared a list of the bindings to be published in a paper along with the new collection of miniatures.

Before completing the paper I wanted to make a further effort to get to the bottom of the Salisbury Hoard, and it was suggested that Andrew Lawson, the Director of Wessex Archaeology, might know something about it. He too had heard the rumours of a massive Salisbury Hoard, including an account of associated miniature shields, but he had no firm evidence. He said that Paul Robinson had acquired some of the items for Devizes Museum. Following my

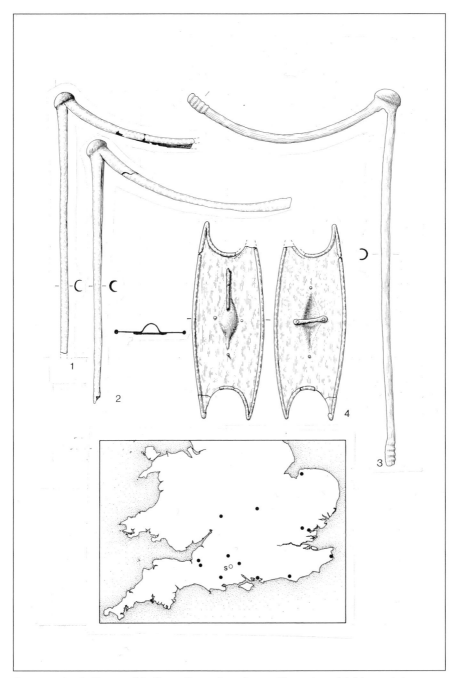

2   1 - 3, Bronze bindings from the edges of Iron Age shields, and 4, Bronze miniature shield with separate binding (scale $\frac{2}{3}$); and a distribution map of the shield bindings (S = Salisbury). Drawn by Stephen Crummy.

earlier contact I had already written to Paul, and sent him copies of drawings and photographs of the miniature shields. The illustrations prompted him to identify a fragment of a miniature shield in the Devizes collection, so I arranged to go down to see it.

I went down to Devizes in August. There was no doubt about the miniature shield: though only half of it survived it was hide-shaped, like most of the shields we had acquired from McAlpine, and unlike any others known. Paul had purchased it from a London dealer, C. J. Martin, along with other items said to be from the Salisbury Hoard. Most were fragments, but there were some complete miniature cauldrons — the first that I had seen. Paul obviously knew more about this hoard than he was prepared to tell me: presumably he had been given information in confidence. But he did confirm the story that the Salisbury Hoard, otherwise known as the 'Dorchester' or 'South Wiltshire' hoard, had comprised 1500 bronze objects that had been removed from the site in a wheelbarrow. He had instigated some research by persuading Joan Taylor (Liverpool University) to have soil samples and surface corrosion products examined. An early flat axe and a much later socketed spearhead had been selected because of their disparate dates, and significant differences between the two sets of surface accretions had been noted. Perhaps artefacts from more than one hoard had been confused in the trade. If 1500 artefacts had indeed been buried in the one deposit it would be the second largest Bronze Age hoard ever found in Britain, and its supposed date range was quite without parallel.

Paul Robinson also knew of the existence of photographs of some artefacts from the hoard, including one that suggested another link with McAlpine. In 1987 the Ashmolean Museum had held a temporary exhibition of selected objects from the McAlpine collection and published a catalogue entitled *Antiquities from the Collection of the Lord McAlpine of West Green* edited by Arthur MacGregor. It was a curious work of limited academic value: there were lots of antiquities, some quite interesting, but few were provenanced and some had circulated in the antiquities trade for years. Various members of the Ashmolean's staff had made contributions, including Andrew Sherratt who had written introductory paragraphs to the major sections. It was noted that 'details relating to place of purchase and known provenance were taken from a hand-list previously prepared by Maurice Braham', the antiquities dealer whose name had already been mentioned in the context of the miniature shields. Most of the items in the catalogue were single finds, but seven 'groups' were distinguished and some had been sampled and analysed by Peter Northover, the Oxford archaeological metallurgist. The first, and largest, of the seven groups, 'said to have been recovered from a well in the Gloucestershire area', comprised 32 Bronze Age antiquities, with three more 'supposedly associated'. Northover and Sherratt doubted that the group was a single find, but 'it nevertheless contains a certain amount of undoubted hoard material and may well be a conflation of material from at least two hoards'.

Paul Robinson said that artefacts from McAlpine's Group 1 hoard, 'from the Gloucestershire area', were included on a photograph that he had seen — a photograph of part of the Salisbury Hoard. Until now I had not pressed McAlpine about the provenance of his antiquities, knowing that there was little chance of success. Indeed, his attitude towards provenance came over clearly in the Ashmolean's catalogue — it was of relatively minor importance. But if he had really handled two major consignments from the Salisbury Hoard (Group 1 and the miniature shields) then he must have some useful information. On returning from Devizes I sent him a long letter. I gave my reasons for supposing that the miniature shields and his Group 1 had the same provenance in a large hoard: 'if it really included all the types ascribed to it then it is quite unique and most important'. I knew that he had little interest in provenance, but 'this collection, and the site that it came from, is too important and I must make every effort to get more information. It must be possible to reconstruct the chain of dealing, to locate the original finder, and explain to him the importance of his discovery. We shall never be able to reconstruct the entire find, but we should be able to learn a lot more about the site.' There was no response.

About this time the Salisbury Hoard came up in conversation with Barbara Green (Norwich Castle Museum), who thought that one of her contacts, Peter Day, might know something about it. Barbara had known Peter since he was a schoolboy, when he had been a metal detecting enthusiast who had submitted artefacts to her at the museum. Peter Day had later moved to the south coast, where he had done some dealing, and had then returned to East Anglia. We had had a recent contact with him, about an Iron Age brooch, so we had his address, and I decided to write.

Peter Day's reply was a real breakthrough because he knew more about the hoard than any of my previous contacts. He had acquired objects from the 'Dorchester' alias Salisbury Hoard in the antiquities trade and made some progress in researching them, information that he had passed to Andrew Lawson in confidence. Some of his pieces were acquired by Devizes Museum, and the rest he photographed and then sold in the trade. The only items that he had retained were three bronze ferrules, enclosed with his letter, that he had purchased for £15 to stop them being 'lost'. He confirmed that the miniature shields were definitely part of the hoard, and all except one were disposed of by a Lincolnshire dealer. The only one that Peter had seen was hide-shaped and decorated: it had been retained by the finder but subsequently sold, possibly to someone in the Bristol area. He said that he had related the story as he knew it to Andrew Lawson some time ago, and had very little to add, although he did have photographs of other pieces from the hoard, seen more recently in the trade. He now thought that the hoard was found in or near Bemerton, $1\frac{1}{2}$ miles west of Salisbury. He had been told that about 1000 artefacts had been found in a pit dug into the chalk. On the top were socketed axes, and the hoard ranged from Early Bronze Age flat axes down to Iron Age 'trappings', so it was spread over almost 2000 years which seemed quite incredible. No items of silver, gold or iron had been found. Peter offered every assistance, but he was 'not happy to hear about it again after the nastiness following my innocent amateur researches'. The 'nastiness' he did not explain.

So I contacted Andrew Lawson, to pass on the latest information and to enquire whether he or any of his colleagues was actively pursuing the hoard. If not, I suggested that we should gather together all available evidence at the British Musuem: the find was obviously too important to ignore. We had started by seeking a context for the miniature shields, but now we were beginning to research the entire hoard. Some time later I saw Andrew in the Museum. We had a long chat and he offered to collate all the evidence that he had gathered and send it to us. It eventually arrived in October 1991 — about a year after Peter Day's letter — but, then, both Andrew and I had other priorities at the time.

I also followed up Peter Day's reference to a decorated miniature shield kept separately from the rest and sold to someone perhaps in the Bristol area. Was this one of ours, or was there another at large? I wrote to Lord McAlpine and reminded him that he had acquired the shields from several different sources — was the 'Bristol' shield one of them? This query provoked a response — the only letter I had had from McAlpine: 'I have spent some time researching the "decorated shield" from the Bristol area that you mention in your letter. I am pleased to tell you that it forms part of the collection you have in your possession.'

Peter Day's 'ferrules' were curious objects and I had not seen their like, but I suggested that the Museum should purchase them for a small sum - it would be cheaper to buy them than record them. He agreed, and offered them for the £15 that they had cost him. And he sent a couple of photographs of pieces from the hoard and offered to lend others. At the same time he provided two names: John Fowler (he gave his address in Exmouth), a collector who had some items from the hoard, and Brian Cavill, a Swindon photographer who had taken a complete set of photographs for the finder. There the matter had to rest for a while because at the time, November 1990, I was digging up hoards at Snettisham (p. 146): that excavation, and its aftermath, occupied most of my time for the next few months and the Salisbury Hoard had to take a back seat.

The Snettisham Treasure Trove inquest was held on 7 March 1991, and a massive 'Celts' exhibition opened at Venice later that month. David Keys, a journalist who wrote for *The Independent*, had been on the phone over both matters and that prompted me to put him to work on the Salisbury Hoard. I told him as much as I knew — keeping Peter Day's name out of it — and said that there was a good story in it for him if he could get some more information. He had a lot of contacts in the archaeological world, and he had heard of the story before, but I was able to give him further details. Some time later, in the middle of 1991, he phoned back with more facts. At the time I had no idea of his sources, but subsequently I guessed that one was Peter Northover. According to Keys the hoard had been found at Whitcombe, near Dorchester, and had moved in the antiquities trade from Bournemouth to Portobello Road; then a substantial part had gone to Jonathan Rosen, a collector in the United States. Rosen had it for three or four years before returning some or all to C. J. Martin, the London dealer from whom Devizes Museum had acquired pieces. The Lincolnshire dealer who had handled the hoard was John Cummings, of Grantham: Keys had phoned him but he had been reluctant to talk about it. Keys also said that Nigel Mills had about 20 items from the hoard but I got no response when I wrote to Nigel.

In October 1991 Andrew Lawson sent the results of his researches: an account of what he had been told about the Salisbury Hoard together with a list of 288 artefacts compiled from information provided mainly by Peter Day and Paul Robinson, and a collection of photocopies of photographs including the one that Paul had told me about, with artefacts from McAlpine's Group 1. Andrew had heard of the hoard in the first week of July 1985, when he had been contacted by Peter Day, an acquaintance from the days when they both worked in Norfolk. Peter had bought a collection of bronzes, and wanted a professional opinion, but he emphasised that it was a matter of the strictest confidence (and Andrew's report to me was clearly marked CONFIDENTIAL). They met at Peter's house at Bognor Regis where it was explained that, although Peter was sympathetic to archaeologists' interests, he did not want them to know of this particular discovery because the finders wanted to keep it secret. He seemed to know the finders (Andrew got the impression that there were two or even three of them) but he himself had not been involved. Peter was able to list 53 items from a hoard of about 100 pieces found early in 1985 about 3 miles north-east of Dorchester. He produced 17 black-and-white photographs of items in his collection, a polaroid shot of 12 pieces taken at Seaby's on 26 July (only two days before his meeting with Andrew), and extracts from two of Seaby's catalogues. Andrew could not accept that all the artefacts had come from one hoard because they were so varied in date and condition, but he failed to convince Peter who was adamant that it was a single deposit.

Subsequently Peter Day had written to Andrew to say that he had met the finder of the hoard and 'I now know as much about it as we are likely to learn in the absence of the hoard items or photographs of the whole hoard. I am assured that the latter do not exist however as only a selection were photographed and there is no chance of getting a copy of these.' He provided information in confidence, again, as 'I do not wish to compromise the trust I have built up with the finder. I do feel however that this was probably the most important hoard of such material ever found in England and any facts I can salvage for posterity must be worth the effort. I can confirm that it came from near Salisbury and was partially plough-damaged on arable land and not on a scheduled site, hill fort or similar such area. The bulk of the items remained at the time of finding *in situ* in a pit cut into the underlying chalk of the valley side.' Between the two letters Peter's information had changed from a Dorchester provenance to one near Salisbury.

Andrew had then contacted the museums at Dorchester, Salisbury, and Devizes to ask if they knew of a recent hoard. Roger Peers, at Dorchester, responded with references to bronzes from a votive deposit in north Dorchester advertised in Seaby's Antiquities Forum. In December 1986 Peers wrote again to say that John Allan at the Exeter Museum had sent photographs of 12 objects from a so-called hoard brought in to his museum by John Fowler, of Exmouth. The hoard was said to have come from near Dorchester and had been purchased from a dealer in Grantham. The 12 objects were among those recorded by Peter Day.

Andrew had also examined four pins and two razors that Peter Day had left to be recorded at Norwich Castle Museum. They too were said to be from the hoard. He also saw a collection of 33 fragmentary bronzes bought at an antique shop in Arundel, Sussex. They had been purchased by Jeremy Knight (Littlehampton Museum) for £15 and said to have been in the shop for about 18 months (ie since early 1985) but found perhaps as early as 1981–2. It was thought that they came from Norfolk, and in January 1988 they were passed to the Norwich Castle Museum for curation. Andrew considered that these pieces might well have belonged to a hoard, but it was unlikely to be from Norfolk. He saw close parallels in the Salisbury Hoard, and the collection was eventually transferred to Devizes Museum.

Andrew's report concluded with a word of warning. He felt that we should be cautious about publicising the find, because Peter Day was quite upset about it, and had even felt threatened in some way. As was obvious from my contact with him, Peter was trapped between the secrecy that surrounded the discovery and his knowledge that the hoard was extremely important. David Keys had been pressing for information about the hoard, but Andrew had stonewalled because he was worried about betraying Peter Day's confidence. I told him about my contact with Keys, who had been able to add names (Cummings, Rosen and Martin) that had not appeared in Andrew's report. I also reassured him that Peter Day had independently spoken (or written) to several other archaeologists about this find.

Andrew also sent a copy of his report to Paul Robinson, who provided some amendments. Paul claimed that little of his information about the hoard had come from Peter Day, although he had known him for many years. He had obtained the photograph of part of the hoard (including some of McAlpine's Group 1) 'from a local North Wilts friend/treasure hunter who had acquired it at the Coinex Fair in November 1984 in London, where objects from the hoard were being offered for sale'. He knew that there were 19 bowls (miniature cauldrons) in the hoard, and Devizes Museum had acquired five of them, all from Peter Day.

In January 1992 we got a further communication from Peter Day, in response to a letter sent in December 1990. Peter was not a particularly prompt correspondent. He enclosed 28 black-and-white and 17 colour photographs for us to copy. Most of them had been included in the photocopies submitted by Andrew Lawson, but 15 of the black-and-white photographs were new to us.

When Peter Day wrote again, to thank us for the return of these photographs, he suggested that we should contact Brian Cavill, the photographer (and metal detector enthusiast) said to have recorded the entire hoard. Peter had tried writing to him but had had no reply, and I was no more successful. I wrote to him at the address provided and then at another address that one of our photographers had found in a professional journal: both letters were returned by the Post Office.

I had been researching the Salisbury Hoard for more than two years, and it seemed that the leads were beginning to dry up. It was frustrating to have identified people who had the information we needed, but to be unable to persuade them to tell all that they knew. However, we had made progress. There was a strong suggestion that we were dealing with an extremely large hoard with an incredible date range from about 2000 BC to 200 BC - something quite without parallel. But the archaeological world would not accept this lightly; we needed proof. The alternative theory, which would be easier to accept, was that several different hoards had been conflated by metal detectorists. One could indeed have been discovered at or near Salisbury, another at Dorchester, and perhaps a third in Gloucestershire. There were other unknown factors. Above all, why was Peter Day so nervous? We were beginning to think that there might be a body in the case!

Months went by without a hint of progress, and then came a mighty step forward, out of the blue, with a telephone call from David Keys on Monday, 7 December 1992.

2. John of Salisbury

Over the week-end one of the finders had telephoned David Keys and provided him with lots of details. To end nearly eight years of secrecy by talking to a member of the press seemed odd. The finder explained that there had been only the one deposit, including artefacts of different periods with a total weight of about 1cwt (50kg). There were thousands of objects, mostly in fragments, but several hundred complete or substantially complete. They were in a pit about 3ft deep (he could reach the bottom without getting in to it), 2ft by 3ft across, cut into chalk, half-way up a hill. He would not give the precise location but it was within four or five miles of Salisbury but not in the direction of Stonehenge (David had pressed him on this point). It had been found seven years previously, and the finder had returned to the site annually and was still finding things in the plough-soil — but everything had been scattered from the one deposit.

The artefacts had been deposited in an orderly way: first a dagger, then palstaves, followed by chisels and gouges, daggers, and then axes at the top. The miniature shields were definitely part of the deposit, and one of them much finer than the others had been sold separately for £4000. The finder then listed the artefacts still in his possession: ten more or less complete pieces came from the pit, and two had been found in the plough-soil; there were also about 100 fragments, which he kept in an old sock! The finder also had a collection of between 12 and 20 photographs of all the artefacts found in the hoard, and he had the negatives for them.

He told David that the original find had been sold for £10,500 and the proceeds split three ways between the two finders and the farmer. But that was when they were green and did not know the value of things. He wanted all the remaining artefacts, and the photographs, to go to a museum; he was prepared to sell them for £20,000. David insisted that he would not buy information, but said that he would act as an honest broker and put the finder in touch with a possible source of funds. The finder would meet neither David Keys nor anyone else, but would arrange for the collection to be viewed, and would give the purchaser a complete account of the find, including the precise provenance. He would not give his name or his telephone number, but when David insisted that he could not remain totally anonymous they settled on calling him 'John'. David gave him my telephone number.

The following day, or perhaps the day after that, 'John' telephoned me at the office. At first I thought he was a crank, and I tried to pass him on: I told him that I did not deal with Bronze Age antiquities, he'd got the wrong man. Then the penny dropped and I realised that I was speaking to the man who had phoned David. He did not want to talk then — he was obviously in a public place because there was a very noisy background, so I gave him my home telephone number and told him to ring me any evening.

'John' telephoned me at home on the following Friday evening. He spoke openly about all the finds but was obviously worried about legal ownership. He had had permission to detect and indeed the farmer had shared in the proceeds when the bulk of the artefacts were sold, but that farmer had since retired (the find was made in February 1985) and 'John' had had no recent contact with him. The new farmer had also given permission for detecting, but 'John' did not know whether either of them was a tenant or a freeholder. He would try to find out, and I assured him that we ought to be able to find a way round problems of ownership. We agreed that he must be the rightful owner of the photographs. He seemed keen to continue the conversation and gave me more details of the finds. The miniature shields definitely belonged to the find and there had been 15 of them: I told him that we had 22, which puzzled him. He would not name the purchaser of the best one, but described it and it sounded like the finest of those acquired from McAlpine. 'John' then read out a complete list of finds: 15 votive shields; 28 cups (miniature cauldrons); 4 chapes; 13 pins; 2 pairs of tweezers; 5 razors; 1 strap buckle; 5 pendants; 1 brooch (he described it in detail, and it did not sound like a brooch); 3 circular discs; 8 punches; 5 miscellaneous decorated pieces; 5 funnels; 6 studs; 88 socketed axes, with a high tin content, and 3 similar but larger; 18 loop and socketed axes and 4 smaller of the same kind; 2 hammers; 7 palstaves; 1 large and 9 small flanged axes; 22 chisels; 17 gouges; 1 punch; 12 flat axes; 31 spear- or arrow-heads; 39 dagger blades; and 1 sickle. He gave more details of two of the artefacts that he had retained: a dagger, 30cm (12in) long with an open socketed handle in the form of an inverted Y; and a decorated bronze pommel, 4cm ($1\frac{5}{8}$in) diameter.

I said that I very much wanted to see the remaining artefacts and the photographs, but he was adamant that he would not bring them to the British Museum. I offered to go anywhere to see them, and he suggested Salisbury. Did I know the Red Lion, in the centre of the town? I didn't, but I was sure that I could find it easily. So we arranged to meet there on the following Monday, between 10.30 and 11.00, in a bar off the reception area called, ominously, the Lion's Den Bar. So that he would recognise me I had to describe myself which caused much amusement to Tony Pacitto, who was listening to my end of all this — he was staying with us while we were surveying at Essendon (p. 145). As a final touch, and in honour of the contact established by David Keys, I said that I would carry a copy of *The Independent*.

On the Monday I went to Salisbury by train and arrived early, filling in time looking in an antiques market on the road from the Railway Station. I walked past the Red Lion, a large and ancient establishment with thirteenth-century origins according to the sign outside. It had been a coaching inn, and the main entrance was through the courtyard. Still in good time, I did a circuit of the surrounding streets and got back to the Red Lion just after 10.30. The main entrance was in the bottom right-hand corner of the courtyard, an unimpressive door leading to a fairly small reception area. I was about to go up to the desk for directions when 'John' came up to me — 'Ian Stead?' — it was probably *The Independent* under my arm rather than my description. He took me into a coffee bar just off the reception area — the Lion's Den Bar was presumably the licensed bar in the opposite direction. It was a long low timber-framed room with a serving area beyond a massive black oak fire-place. They were quite busy, but 'John' led me to a corner table just inside the door, and we sat together on a long and comfortably upholstered bench with our backs to the wall. He ordered coffee, and we started to chat. He was probably in his late 30s, 5ft 8in or a little less, dark haired and balding, with blue-grey eyes, confident and friendly, divorced and with children. He lived and metal detected in the vicinity of Salisbury, but was not allowed to work on big estates, so there was only a limited amount of land available to him.

I had brought some photographs and photocopies, including the set that Andrew Lawson had sent me. 'John' wanted to see all this before he showed me his collection. The miniature shields were certainly part of the find, and he agreed that there were about 22 of them: he had said 15 because he had been confused by the photographs — some fragments had not been photographed. He wanted to know how much we had paid for them but at the time, quite genuinely, I could not remember. McAlpine's 'Gloucestershire' group was certainly part of his hoard, but he did not recognise the next group that I produced. It was a selection from the 'Batheaston' Hoard (see p. 120) — a deliberate plant — and his reaction supported our suspicions that 'Batheaston' and Salisbury were two separate hoards. He went through all Andrew's photocopies and eventually accepted the lot, though at first he rejected four of the pins, perhaps because they were recorded as drawings and not photographs. He was annoyed when he saw the group photograph **(Colour plate 4)**: that was a copy of one of his. It could have come from one source only and he would telephone someone about it that night. Then 'John' dipped into the plastic bag that he had brought, an ordinary supermarket shopping-bag, and produced his photographs. There were 16 of them, all in colour, and the main group views were in a large format, 200 by 162mm (8 by $6\frac{1}{2}$ in). Their quality was excellent, and the range of antiquities was amazing **(Colour plates 2–5, and 16)**. I sketched one or two of them, including a curious moustache-like object subsequently located in McAlpine's catalogue.

Then he produced his artefacts, all packed in old socks, one within a Lloyds Bank money bag and the others in a plastic bag. There were eight 'really nice' objects, seven others and a sockful of scraps. The 'really nice' objects were: the dagger with socketed handle, squarish section, two rivet-holes (I made a rough sketch); the 'brooch', a curious object (also sketched); a ring, circular section, enclosing openwork 'Y' decoration (sketched); a socketed pommel, fine dark green patina, possibly from a sword (but it did not belong to 'John's' dagger) — he gave me a photograph of it and a sketch that he had made; a long narrow socketed axe; another socketed axe, as cast, not cleaned up; a razor; and a fine and quite small flat axe, with slight flanges and a slight cross-ridge. For the rest there were two small socketed spear-heads, two miniature cauldrons, a pin, a tanged chisel and the tip of the dagger. This dagger-tip was the first object that he had found, and he said that most of the daggers had been deliberately broken. The bag of scrap included many pieces of 'high tin' socketed axes, some bits of once molten waste including part of a miscast socketed axe, and part of a miniature shield.

I was very impressed, and said that the British Museum would like to acquire both the artefacts and the photographs. The first stage would be to show them to my colleagues and agree a valuation, and then to put them before the Trustees. There was a meeting of the Trustees next month, 22 January, perhaps I could borrow them for the occasion? But he would not let me take them away, would not himself bring them to the Museum, and said that the asking price was not negotiable. He wanted £20,000 for the lot, and would not sell the photographs separately. He was well aware of the significance of his hoard, and was keen that it should go to a museum, especially the British Museum. I asked if he knew Peter Clayton, and he thought that he had spoken to him on the phone, so I suggested that we might be able to arrange a meeting at Seaby's, and that seemed to suit him.

I pressed him on the matter of ownership, but did not get anywhere. He did not know who owned the land and was not interested in finding out. The farmer, now retired, who had given permission for the work and who had shared in the original sale, had agreed to 'John' retaining the collection now on offer. He would not reveal the site of the discovery, not even the parish, saying that the parishes were so small that they would lead us quickly to the farm. I threw in the name 'Bemerton', which Peter Day had suggested, and got a response that was perhaps a little too blank. He could not understand why we were now so keen on knowing the provenance when we had bought from McAlpine without question. In any case, he was in no particular hurry to sell and already had another offer for £20,000: we were going to have to make the running, and it would not be easy.

Returning to the hoard itself, 'John' confirmed that everything had been found in the one pit, and added that the socketed axes had been neatly arranged, end to end and spread fan-wise. I left after he had promised to phone again in the New Year. He stayed behind and paid the bill.

Shortly after this meeting Peter Northover phoned to say that he had heard about another group of objects from the Salisbury Hoard in the possession of a Scottish farmer who had submitted them to the National Museums of Scotland at Edinburgh for an opinion. The farmer had bought a larger collection, but had sold the rest. Peter described one of the pieces as a non-utilitarian 'model' socketed gouge. He said that he had spoken to David Keys who had told him that I now had a lot more information, so I described my meeting with 'John of Salisbury'. Later I spoke to Alison Sheridan, at Edinburgh, and she confirmed that they had the collection and were recording it. She would send me a set of photographs.

'John' telephoned me at home before Christmas. He was worried. He had made enquiries and been warned to avoid direct contact with the British Museum because they were 'over-zealous'. He wanted the finds and photographs to come to us, but it would be better to do it the same way as before, as we had acquired the miniature shields, with a dealer as an intermediary. I pointed out that he would certainly get less money if he went through a dealer, but he said he would be happy to arrange it on a percentage basis. This was the first indication that the private collector who had offered £20,000 was indeed a fiction. However, I pursued the idea of a meeting at Seaby's, and he seemed happy to go along with it. I had already discussed it with Peter Clayton and Ian Longworth (Keeper of Prehistoric and Romano-British Antiquities at the British Museum). I wanted Ian to be able to assess both 'John' and the antiquities at first hand — and I had some dates that both of them could manage. 'John' noted the dates and said that he would phone again after Christmas. I also asked for a written account of the discovery, the archaeology of the discovery, and he said that he would think about it.

I contacted Paul Robinson, to keep him abreast of developments, and in the course of the conversation he said that he had been offered McAlpine's 'Gloucestershire' hoard by a dealer called Nicholas Wright. Up to that point I had assumed that the 'Gloucestershire' hoard was part of McAlpine's private collection rather than his dealing collection. Why else would it have appeared in the Ashmolean Museum's catalogue? The asking price had been reasonable, but the published Gloucestershire provenance was too much of a problem, even for Paul. Provincial museums have clearly defined collecting areas, and Devizes could not extend much beyond Wiltshire. Wright, Paul said, was Michael Tippett's agent, and that rang a bell. He was the man who had brought in the ox-head fitting that I had subsequently borrowed from McAlpine, the piece that had been stolen from the Ryedale Folk Museum. I looked back through our files, found Wright's telephone number and rang him.

Nicholas Wright confirmed that he had offered the 'Gloucestershire' hoard to Paul Robinson some months before, acting on commission from McAlpine. As far as he knew it was still on offer: were we interested? Later he phoned back to say that most of the pieces were still available, but four had been sold; I took the opportunity to get him to add three more pieces almost certainly from the Salisbury Hoard though not listed with the 'Gloucestershire' hoard, including the 'moustache' object that featured in one of 'John's' photographs. That brought the total to 31 objects, and they were on offer for £5000. Wright came in with them in January 1993, and left them so that I could show them to colleagues and get them photographed **(Colour plate 6)**. While he was in we went through the McAlpine catalogue and I pointed out an anvil that Stuart Needham had spotted on one of Andrew Lawson's photocopies. Wright thought that it was still on offer, and subsequently he brought it in.

We met 'John' at Seaby's on 20 January 1993. Seaby's had moved since my last visit, and Ian Longworth and I managed to get lost en route, so 'John' was there first and the antiquities were already spread out on Peter Clayton's table. 'John' told Ian the story that I had heard at Salisbury, and we all looked at the photographs: Ian was very noncommittal, so I took on an enthusiastic role. The one new fact that emerged was that the photographs had been taken on the evening of the discovery, and that Brian — presumably Brian Cavill — was there. I had taken along three of the artefacts submitted by Nicholas Wright. 'John' recognised two of them but not the third, though he could not be positive that it had not been in the hoard. 'John' still refused to name the landowner, and without that information we could make no progress. If he gave me the name I could approach him on the basis that we had heard of a find from an unknown site on his land and we knew the finder only as 'John'. If the landowner would cooperate it would be plain-sailing but if he declined then 'John' had lost nothing because the site was still unknown and he himself had not been identified. He said that he would think about it and phone me. I pressed on and said that our aim would be not only to identify the site but to re-excavate it: he seemed interested in the idea and said that he could definitely locate it to within an area equivalent to the size of Peter's room. If we were going to pursue this idea, the site could not be excavated until the autumn because there was a crop on it - another potentially useful snippet of information. One other fact that emerged at this meeting was that 'John' had located the hoard with a C-scope metal detector that he had had for quite some time.

Before we left, 'John' took the fragment of miniature shield from his sockful of scrap, and gave it to me 'as an act of good faith' because I had shown so much interest in it. On the way back to the Museum it occurred to me that the only other part-shield that I had seen was the fragment in Devizes Museum. I wondered if the two would join, and as soon as I got back I looked out the photograph that Paul Robinson had given me. There was no doubt about it. The Devizes fragment was rather more than half, 'John's' fragment was much smaller (the ends were broken) but the breaks across the middle definitely matched. The one fragment had been part of the collection purchased from C.J. Martin, and according to David Keys' information it had been across the Atlantic and back, the other had never left the finder. Two significant strands in the story of the Salisbury Hoard had come together.

Paul Robinson offered to bring his fragment when he next came in: he had to deliver some coins in the near future. Eventually I had the two pieces photographed together, and presented Paul with 'John's' fragment to join the piece already accessed in his collection **(Colour plate 7)**.

Peter Clayton had continued his discussion with 'John' after Ian and I had left Seaby's. He had gathered that the main cause for secrecy now was 'John's' fear that his ex-wife would hear about the proposed sale and want her share of it; he also learnt that 'John' was currently unemployed, though not in urgent need of the money. As for valuation, Peter believed that he really did have a genuine offer from elsewhere, though he doubted that it was £20,000. 'John' was setting the high value mainly on the strength of the decorated pommel which he was comparing with a piece that brought a high price at Christie's in 1982. Peter couldn't recall it, but I thought he must mean the Saxthorpe horn-cap that the British Museum bought at Christie's in 1984. However, the horn-cap is very different, much larger and finely decorated with Celtic art. 'John' was to phone Peter with details of this 'parallel' in the evening. With regard to the problem of provenance, Peter had devised a formula that 'John' had accepted. At the time of the sale, 'John' would hand over a sealed envelope with full details of the precise find-spot: the envelope would then remain unopened for six months. But this was not at all what we wanted, and I said that we would have to take a much firmer line.

That same evening 'John' phoned me and gave his version of the meeting, which was exactly the same as Peter's. I did not discuss valuation and did not mention the Saxthorpe horn-cap. He was very taken with Peter's compromise on provenance and said that we couldn't get on to the site for six months in any case, because of the crop. He gave the impression that he was not going to move from this position, so I said that I would put it to Ian Longworth. The most that I could manage was to insist that any sketch plan was very detailed, and to ask for a full written account of the discovery to be included in the envelope.

The following day I spoke to George Morris, the Museum's

Secretary, about the Statute of Limitations which was another matter raised by Peter Clayton, and I had to explain the background to the case. George checked with the Treasury Solicitor and established that limitation normally extended for six years, but in the case of theft there is no limitation. If a stolen item is subsequently sold then the limitation is six years from that sale. The Treasury Solicitor would advise against any purchase until we had full details of provenance, and was particularly worried about the Museum's image, especially when he heard that the press (David Keys) was in the picture. I went back to Peter Clayton, who decided to write a formal letter to the Museum, a letter that he could also show to 'John', setting out 'John's' position.

Meanwhile, 'John' telephoned me to say that he had been thinking hard about the matter and had decided that he did not want to proceed with the deal that Peter Clayton had proposed. But I kept him talking, indeed it seemed that he wanted to keep talking, and we made some progress. For the first time he admitted that he had not had permission to work in that field. The 'farmer' who had shared in the proceeds of the initial sale was in fact a farm labourer, and the landowner, who knew nothing of the discovery, was 'a right bastard'. That did not worry me in the least, because I was quite used to dealing with 'right bastards'. I also pointed out that we had established other lines of enquiry: for instance, we knew all about Brian Cavill. This obviously surprised him, but he agreed that Cavill had taken the photographs, though he had not been involved in the excavation. Come what may, David Keys would write his story, I said. 'John' replied that I would have to stop him. But how could I? 'John' had given him all the facts.

We then spoke about valuation, and I disillusioned him about the comparison between his pommel and the Saxthorpe horn-cap. Ian Longworth thought that his pommel was worth no more than £500, and none of the other pieces on offer was individually worth more than £100. 'John' said that a dealer had offered five figures for the dagger, so I advised him to accept it because there was no way that we would give him anything like that. At the moment we had a far bigger selection from his hoard on offer for £5000, and we would be unlikely to pay as much as that for it. He did not seem to be too worried by these figures, and said that the price was negotiable, so I suggested that any negotiations should be carried out through Peter Clayton. Subsequently he contacted Peter and said that he wanted to sell his antiquities in the trade.

The news that 'John' did not have title to the Salisbury Hoard, that it had been stolen from an unknown landowner who was quite unaware of its existence, altered our position significantly. For one thing, we could no longer contemplate purchasing McAlpine's 'Gloucestershire' hoard: it too had been stolen by 'John'. I explained the problem to Nicholas Wright, who was intrigued by the story and sympathised with our position. He called in and collected the antiquities, and I wondered if we would ever see them again. It was maddening to have to let them go.

One Saturday in February, I went to a Coin Fair at the Cumberland Hotel, where I had arranged to meet Peter Clayton. It was a fair attended by several antiquities dealers, and it occurred to me that I might meet up with 'John'. Instead I met John Cummings, the Grantham dealer said to have been the first to handle the hoard. He had a double stall with lots of coins and a few antiquities on one corner. Peter introduced me, saying that I was from the British Museum, and I examined the antiquities. I asked if he had anything from the Salisbury Hoard: he had nothing with him, but at home he had three miniature shields like the ones that we had but better decorated. He knew all about our acquisition of the shields. Apart from the three that he had at home he knew of two others, one still with the finder and another that had been taken by the photographer, Brian Cavill, and subsequently sold. He was quite open about his connection with the hoard, which he had bought from the finder. Peter was still with us, and one of us mentioned 'John'. Cummings said that he knew who we were talking about, but 'John' was certainly not the finder. The hoard had been found by a coin dealer from Salisbury. Cummings was confident and talkative. Our miniature shields had certainly been through his hands, and when I referred to the repairs, described them as quite professional, and asked if he knew who had done them, he seemed flattered and took the credit himself. He mentioned Maurice Braham as an intermediary, with the implication that the shields had passed from the finder to Cummings to Braham to McAlpine and then to the British Museum. I didn't really believe that he had more shields, that was probably bravado; certainly there were no more decorated shields on 'John's' photographs. Cummings said that he *might* show them to me, but there was no promise. His story that the finder was a Salisbury coin dealer, who sometimes had a stall at small fairs but not at the Cumberland Hotel, might make some sense if 'John' had first sold to a local dealer who Cummings then assumed to be the finder.

David Miller had a stall at the Cumberland Hotel, too, but he was quite busy and I did not talk to him. I did meet Nigel Mills, who was very affable but did not want to talk about the hoard in that company: he was still sticking to the story that it had been found at Dorchester. Chris Martin was there, and I had a good look at his stall, but he did not know me and we did not speak. I went round all the stalls, but there was no sign of anything from the Salisbury Hoard.

Looking for new approaches to the problem, I spoke to Clare Conybeare, formerly of Salisbury Museum, who knew something of the metal detecting scene in Wiltshire. Clare had been told about the Salisbury Hoard by a Mr Rossiter, of Water Lane, Salisbury, in the spring of 1987. Rossiter had provided some details of the find including mention of a full set of photographs with scales. The hoard had been found in an open field where the landowner had given permission for metal detecting and then withdrawn it. Rossiter was a friend of the finder, and had seemed nervous or frightened: we compared descriptions and it did not seem that Rossiter and 'John' were the same person. Rossiter had said that the finder was a metal detectorist and coin collector, who had been very annoyed to see that Seaby's were selling some of his finds at four times the price that he had got for them.

Another potentially useful contact was Nick Griffiths, an archaeological illustrator who knew quite a few of the Wiltshire metal detectorists and recorded finds for them. He had heard of the Salisbury Hoard but could not recognise my description of 'John'. I mentioned Rossiter, of Water Lane (his full address and telephone number was in the phone book) but again he did not know him. We discussed possible dealers, following my idea that there may have been a local dealer intermediary between 'John' and Cummings, and he mentioned two possibilities. One of them had a shop at the end of Water Lane, where Rossiter lived. On one occasion Nick had been there when a customer was advised not to take finds to Salisbury Museum but to sell direct to the dealer.

Nick Griffiths knew Brian Cavill, who had been seriously ill quite recently with a heart condition, so he questioned him about the Salisbury Hoard. Cavill told him that he had met 'John' on metal detecting expeditions in the Salisbury area. 'John' had phoned him in a panic when he found the hoard and arranged for him to photograph it, but Cavill never saw the site. He gave 'John' the negatives and a set of prints, but retained some prints which he kept locked away. He was not very well and wanted to keep clear of the whole matter. He thought that 'John' lived on the Bemerton Heath Estate, but he would not reveal his real name.

Clare Conybeare wrote with more information about her contact with Rossiter: she had checked her correspondence files and confirmed his address. Rossiter had written to Clare in March 1985, which must have been about the time that the Salisbury Hoard had been discovered, and she enclosed a copy of his letter. He and his friend had wanted to form a metal detecting club in the area. They wanted 'to do properly concerning the codes of conduct' and have a meeting once a month to discuss finds, sites and other archaeological aspects. Clare at that time worked at Salisbury Museum, and Rossiter wanted close cooperation. He said that he was currently unemployed and offered to do voluntary work. Clare had responded saying that if they set up a club she would be willing to talk to them and identify objects, but she stressed that they must abide by a code of practice, keep within the law, and give Salisbury Museum the oportunity to record finds. After that she heard nothing from him until he contacted her in the spring of 1987, as she had previously told me. She emphasised that on that occasion Rossiter had spoken in confidence. I encouraged her to make contact again, and to be quite open about my interest, my contact with 'John' and the importance of the find. Clare had also checked the County Sites and Monuments Record in an attempt to find clues to the site: she sent a map indicating a Roman site just east of the Bemerton Heath Estate, and highlighting two farms in the vicinity: Cowslip Farm, near the Roman remains, and Bemerton Farm, to the south.

Meanwhile 'John' had been on the phone two or three times. Talking to Peter Clayton he had reduced his asking price to £10,000. To me he said that he had heard from a friend that we were no longer interested in acquiring his finds. His friend had heard this from someone at Salisbury Museum. I explained Clare's involvement (he agreed that she was the contact) and said that there must have been a misunderstanding: we really did want to acquire, but first we needed to know the name of the landowner. It seemed that 'John' had not had a direct contact with Clare, so 'John' was certainly not Rossiter. On the other hand I now had a way of contacting 'John' if need be, via Rossiter; hitherto I had had to wait for him to phone me. I mentioned the three shields that Cummings had allegedly kept back, but 'John' said that we had the lot. He agreed with the story that Cavill had taken one of the shields, not a decorated one but one that had been repaired in antiquity. 'John's' original contact with Cummings had been direct, there had been no intermediary dealer. He had seen an advert in *Treasure Hunting* and had had some of Cummings' catalogues. He knew nothing about hoards from the Wylye area (the possible 'Batheaston' site, p. 122), but said that there were quite a few night-hawks from the Bath area operating in south Wiltshire. 'John' still insisted that he would not reveal the site or the name of the landowner. He said that only three people knew the site.

In another phone call 'John' told me that someone in the trade had warned him to have nothing to do with the British Museum, they could not be trusted. 'John' had been advised to back out and burn the photographs. Peter Clayton told me that he had heard from both 'John' and Cummings. Cummings was particularly annoyed at our investigations, so it seemed likely that he was the one who had warned 'John'.

Peter Northover, the Oxford metallurgist, keeps cropping up in this story. He contributed to the Ashmolean's McAlpine catalogue, was one of David Keys' informants, and told me of the Salisbury Hoard antiquities in Edinburgh. Now he passed on the names of two collector/dealers who had had items from the hoard. Jonathan Rosen had had pieces in the USA and then returned them to England. I wrote to him, but got no reply. Robin Symes, a London dealer, had a group of about 30 pieces from the hoard, and Northover was going round to examine them. Apparently Symes had acquired them in the late 1980s and kept them in his private collection.

Meanwhile, I had made my own contact with a collector/dealer. McAlpine had not replied to my last letter, so I phoned Rose Anderson to try to arrange a meeting. It took quite a while, because he spent so much time abroad, but eventually I went round to see him on 30 March 1993, at 10 o'clock in the morning. I arrived in good time and he was not there, so Rose showed me into an inner room with a coal fire and two arm-chairs. I made myself comfortable and was given a coffee. This was the second occasion that I had been in these rooms, though they were not the ones in which I had first seen the miniature shields in 1988. Since then McAlpine had moved up from the second to the fifth floor in the same building, and I noticed that the adjoining door on the fifth floor was labelled 'Maurice Braham', the man who had bought the miniature shields from Cummings. McAlpine kept me waiting a long time, and when he eventually arrived he had to make a phone-call to his wife. Then he settled into the arm-chair opposite me and gave me his full attention for about an hour. Other visitors arrived, but they were made to wait in the outer room with Rose. I had brought a case full of photocopies and photographs, and I gave him a full illustrated account of my investigations. He was really interested and kept questioning me about details. He was vague as to how he had acquired the miniature shields and said that he knew nothing about

Cummings.

McAlpine could not conceive how such a collection could have been assembled in antiquity, and wondered if it could be the result of a relatively recent robbery, but I argued against that. He said that he would do anything he could to help, so I explained our problem. I was almost certain that this was a genuine hoard assembled in antiquity, and as such it was unique and of very great importance. It was vital that we should recover as much information as possible, and assemble as many of the artefacts as we could locate. But now we had every reason to suppose that the hoard had been stolen, and the British Museum could not buy stolen property. I was confident that in due course I could crack this one: it was surely possible to locate the site and negotiate with the landowner. But that would take time, and meanwhile we risked the further dispersal of the antiquities. One way in which McAlpine could help was by retaining his 'Gloucestershire' hoard intact until such a time as we were able to acquire it legally. Another way would be for him to see what 'John' had on offer.

He seemed interested and said that, having already acquired two lots allegedly from this hoard, he would be very interested in contacting 'John' to see what information and antiquities he had. I mentioned 'John's' asking price, now £10,000, which he rightly thought was outrageously high; I gave him Peter Clayton's valuation, £5130 retail (except for the horn-cap), which was more reasonable. But he would have to see the antiquities and hear 'John's' story direct, and that was not going to be easy. I knew how difficult it was to arrange a meeting with McAlpine even in his own rooms, and there was no way that I could persuade him to make an assignment at the Red Lion, Salisbury! So I suggested that Peter Clayton might act as an intermediary and he agreed. Immediately, McAlpine was going over to Venice, but perhaps Clayton could telephone him in about three weeks' time.

At the end of April I was lecturing at York at a conference on Treasure, and the previous speaker was Eamonn Kelly, from the National Museum at Dublin. He had had some fascinating exploits recovering antiquities from treasure hunters and had obtained co-operation from the police in both Ireland and the USA. I discussed my problem with him and his advice was clear: buy the antiquities while there was still the opportunity, and sort out the problems afterwards. I was much tempted to follow this, but the feeling in the British Museum was for a more cautious approach.

Over the next few months I had other priorities, especially the excavation at Essendon (p. 144), but Peter Clayton made repeated efforts to see McAlpine. He established a good contact with Rose, and even dealt in some of their antiquities, but he failed completely to meet McAlpine. Meanwhile, 'John' telephoned at frequent intervals. We were getting nowhere at all. Eventually I phoned Rose to see if I could prompt her to expedite the contact between McAlpine and 'John'. She was well aware of the whole story, Peter Clayton would have given her full details even if McAlpine had not mentioned it, and she had obviously formed a very low opinion of 'John'. Rose was always efficient and helpful, but she had a certain naiveté. She was quite without guile, and I liked her. She had lost patience with Peter's attempts to meet McAlpine and negotiate: if he wanted to make progress (she was quite sharp about it) the way forward was obvious: provide a list of what was on offer and the asking price and she would put it to McAlpine and get a decision. So I went back to Peter, who wrote to McAlpine a formal letter, treating 'John' as Seaby's client. He outlined the case, listed the antiquities on offer and 'John's' asking price, and wondered whether McAlpine still had any interest in the group. If not, 'John' had said that he would disperse his antiquities and destroy his photographs, and Peter was expecting a final telephone call from him at the end of the following week. McAlpine made no response.

A month later, 12 September, 'John' telephoned me for the first time for several weeks. Peter Clayton had given up hope of involving McAlpine, and had advised 'John' to submit the antiquities for auction at Bonham's, where we would have access to borrow them and make sure that they were properly recorded. I supported Peter's advice, and said that we were still interested in acquiring the photographs, and I hoped that we could come to some arrangement. But 'John' wanted everything to go to the British Museum, and if he couldn't do it direct he would prefer to go via a dealer because he knew that we had bought the miniature shields that way. He was employed now, and in no great hurry to sell. I told him that if he wanted to sell to the British Museum he could make one of two moves: either give us the name of the landowner, or sell us the photographs. He said that he would think about it, but the landowner had had trouble with metal detectorists before, and was liable to be vindictive. Cummings had told 'John' that he might well be raided by the 'antiquities police', and advised him to sell his antiquities in the trade and burn the photographs. 'John' did not want to go as far as that, but he had taken the precaution of moving both the antiquities and the photographs from his home.

The following week we took a significant step forward when a letter arrived from Peter Day, in response to one that I had sent more than seven months before! Peter named the finders. 'John' was in fact James Garriock, and he provided his address and telephone number. His colleague was Terry Rossiter, as we already suspected, but Peter did not have his address. Garriock did some dealing in coins, and Peter enclosed one of his coin-lists.

This was real progress. I contacted Andrew Burnett (Keeper of Coins and Medals) but nobody in his Department knew anything of James Garriock. Peter Clayton did not know the name either, but he got a response when he mentioned it to David Miller. Miller said that Garriock was worried about the Salisbury antiquities, and had been very quiet of late. So Garriock was surely our man! I decided to write to him direct, in his capacity as a dealer, saying that I had heard that he had handled antiquities from the so-called Salisbury Hoard. I told him of my contact with a man called 'John', and asked if he could help me in persuading 'John' to reveal the name of the landowner. I knew that he would have to reply because he would know that if I had his address I would also have the telephone number that he had been at pains to keep secret. If I phoned him then I would certainly recognise his voice. He replied a few days later, to say that I must be mistaken: he was a coin dealer, and Bronze Age and Iron Age antiquities were out of his league. He was sorry, but he could not help me. He enclosed a copy of the same coin list that Peter Day had sent me.

One day towards the end of the summer Rose Anderson phoned to enquire if we were interested in any of McAlpine's antiquities. I asked if there had been any recent acquisitions. No. In that case I must have seen everything. She then said that perhaps we might be interested in something for which the asking price had been too high, implying that prices were now open to negotiation. Our only interest was in the 'Gloucestershire/Salisbury' hoard, and we could not do anything about that because we now knew that 'John' had acquired it illegally. She said that some of those pieces had just been submitted for auction. I was shocked. McAlpine had promised to keep that 'Gloucestershire' collection together until such a time as we could acquire it legally. Rose failed to understand why we could not buy it without more ado, but she accepted my argument about its importance and promised to see if McAlpine would withdraw it, though at this late stage he might well have to pay a withdrawal fee. However, he did agree to its removal from the auction and she faxed a list of those items still available, offered for £5000.

In the catalogue for the Christie's (South Kensington) Antiquities Sale for 27 October there was a photograph of Lot 12, 11 antiquities from McAlpine's 'Gloucestershire' hoard. Lot 15 was 'two silvered bronze socketed axe heads' (one illustrated) 'and another similar': the illustrated piece, though unprovenanced, was also from the 'Gloucestershire' hoard. Either McAlpine or the auctioneers had separated the 'silvered' axes in Lot 15 in order to get a better price. Thus antiquities lose their provenances. But both lots had been withdrawn, as we confirmed when one of my colleagues went round to Christie's to see something else.

About this time we received from the Department of National Heritage a proof copy of a list of objects offered for sale by C. J. Martin. Dealers were now required to indicate which of their items might need export licences and Martin had asked if he had overlooked any. Item A138 was a 'British Bronze Age, bronze, high tin content socketed and looped axehead, linear decoration to sides. From the same provenance and ex. Lord McAlpine of West Green. Perfect and superb example — £185.' It was obviously a Salisbury Hoard axe, and the 'same provenance' must have referred back to a previous entry since sold. So there had been at least two Salisbury Hoard objects in his list. I mentioned this axe to Peter Clayton, who offered to borrow it so that we could have a look at it. This incident also drew attention to a further line of research, dealers' lists, but it was some time before I could make any progress on that one.

On Sunday, 26 September, *The Observer* ran a story about metal detectorists, giving the name of David Wood, who was Secretary of the National Council for Metal Detecting. I decided to write to him to pose the problem, and see if he could suggest any way forward. He responded with two letters, one official which said that his organisation would have nothing to do with illegal metal detecting; the other a personal letter that was more helpful. He did not suggest any approach that I had not already tried but he was clearly interested, so I phoned him and we had a long talk. There was no way that he would get involved in talks with 'John', who had broken the metal detectorists' code of practice and put himself beyond the pale. He wondered if the hoard had been found on Crown Estate Commissioners' land, because he thought that they had quite a lot of property in the vicinity of Salisbury. We had had some dealings with the Crown Estate Commissioners having recently excavated on their land in Yorkshire, and though our main contact had since retired Ian Longworth was still in touch with his successor. I discussed it with Ian and decided to write to them on the basis that important antiquities of unknown provenance were being dispersed on the open market. 'Our dilemma is that we cannot buy because we believe them to be stolen, but it would be folly to allow such a very important collection to be still further dispersed. I think that our only way forward is to purchase, and to continue our researches which I am confident will eventually lead to the identification of the landowner, and the precise site. If we allow these pieces to be still further dispersed they will be lost both to the Museum and to the landowner. We know that the site is near Salisbury, perhaps immediately to the south-west of Salisbury, and I have been told that the Crown Estate Commissioners own land in the area. If you are indeed the landowner, would you object if we were to attempt to purchase the antiquities now on offer?'

If they gave a positive response the British Museum could purchase with a relatively clear conscience. We could save the 'Gloucestershire' hoard and perhaps get 'John's' collection as well. In the event the Commissioners responded to say that they had no land in the vicinity, so it was highly unlikely that the antiquities came from the Crown Estate.

Perhaps it was time to try to involve the police. It may seem an obvious step and certainly I had considered it before, but I was afraid that we had too little hard evidence. We would have to deal with the local police which was a real problem because there was still uncertainty about the precise locality, and we did not have a contact. About this time the Coins and Medals Department were involved with the Holborn police, and Andrew Burnett was most impressed with one of their senior detectives, DCI Jack Woods, who was interested in and knowledgeable about antiquities. Andrew offered to mention the Salisbury Hoard to Woods, but we decided that he was unlikely to want to get involved in what seemed likely to be a Wiltshire case.

I discussed the problem with Ian Longworth and Tim Potter — because Tim was then Acting Keeper, Ian having been seconded to direct a major review of security. We concluded that an approach to the police was worth a try: if we did not move rapidly the remaining antiquities would get dispersed and 'John' would destroy the photographs. The Salisbury Hoard was too important to risk losing yet more evidence, and our commitment in terms of time was now very considerable. On the down-side, it might lead to bad publicity and we might lose some useful contacts.

The approach to the police, the official way, would be via our Head of Security, so I went round and had a long chat with Ken Wright, himself a former policeman. Ken listened patiently, but in his opinion we had no sound evidence: it was all hearsay. He was willing to put the case to Jack Woods, but did not think that he could do much. I was disappointed, but Ken's argument was sound. I returned to my room to find a message from Peter Clayton, so I phoned back and told him about my discussion with Ken Wright, who had agreed with Peter's view that there was little point in approaching the police. That was now the Museum's official position, so we were on our own again. I asked Peter to contact 'John', via David Miller, asking 'John' to phone me to arrange one more meeting.

I had no sooner put down the phone than Andrew Burnett rang. He had just been talking to Jack Woods and had mentioned the Salisbury Hoard. Woods was interested, and wanted to talk to me.

3. The Arrests

Jack Woods visited on Thursday, 14 October, and I told him my tale. He was intrigued with the case, seemed to approve of the way I had handled it, and thought that he could help. He asked if I could fix up a meeting with 'John': I had set that in motion already, though not with the intention of a police involvement. He wanted it to be at the end of the following week, to give him time to make preparations. He was a little unsure of his standing, because the crime had been committed outside his area, but he thought that on the one hand the precise site was sufficiently vague — Salisbury, Dorchester or Gloucestershire — and on the other he might be able to operate in conjunction with the Art and Antiques Squad. It had been my intention to take Stuart Needham along to the meeting with 'John', because he was the authority on Bronze Age antiquities. Jack toyed with the idea of replacing Stuart with one of his men. Jack himself was impossible, a big man, every inch a policeman. But we might have to have quite a long conversation, so any substitute would have to be given a crash course in Bronze Age antiquities. Clearly it would be better to take Stuart, and I was sure that he would be willing, though he was away that day so I could not check.

'John' telephoned on the Friday night as requested, soon after I got home. I told him that there had been developments and I thought that we could make some progress. First, McAlpine was splitting up his collection, and unless we acted quickly his part of the hoard would be dispersed. Second, Ian Longworth had been seconded to another post and I had a new boss, Tim Potter. Longworth had always played the villain in the piece, far too sceptical: 'John' had successfully convinced me, but we'd always needed a lot more evidence to persuade Longworth. Potter was different, thought that we had spent far too much time on this matter, and wanted to clear it up quickly. It was the perfect cover story: the essential facts were true, and they could be checked. I suggested that the way forward was to meet again in Salisbury, at the Red Lion. I would bring Stuart who would be able to assess 'John's' bronzes and compare photographs of McAlpine's antiquities so that we could be sure that they were all from the Salisbury Hoard. I did not know Stuart's movements beyond the fact that he was not in on Monday. 'John' suggested a meeting one afternoon, say 2 o'clock, towards the end of the week, perhaps Thursday or Friday, or alternatively the Thursday or Friday of the following week. He would need a day's notice in order to gather the things together, because he had moved them from his home, as he had told me before. I had to talk to Stuart, so I asked him to phone me again on the Tuesday.

On Monday I put Stuart in the picture. Jack Woods had arranged to visit me with one of his colleagues from the Antiques Squad on the Tuesday, and he had agreed that Stuart and Ian Longworth should be involved. We met in Ian's room; Jack Woods came with a Detective Sergeant, Pete Basnett, and Tony Russell from the Antiques Squad arrived later. We agreed to set up the meeting with 'John' for the coming Friday. I was keen to have it as soon as possible, partly because it was going to be such a dominating issue — the longer it was delayed the more people might get to know of it. But also, if we were not meeting him until early afternoon and there was a possiblility that he might show us the site, then we wanted as much daylight as possible, and this was the last week before British Summer Time ended. I was also thinking ahead to a possible excavation. Having had recent digs at Snettisham in late November and December I did not want to repeat the experience. In the afternoon Pete Basnett took a long statement from me, which continued for much of the following morning. Then Ian and I went along to see George Morris, who was worried that the Director knew nothing about the matter (but he was away that day). George found the idea of the trap rather distasteful, but perhaps necessary.

'John' phoned as arranged on the Tuesday evening, later than before. The Friday meeting was fine, but he wanted it slightly later, say 2.30. I agreed, because that would suit the police better as well. He still insisted that he wanted £10,000 for his antiquities and photographs, and said that if we agreed the price we could take the antiquities away with us. I thought his price was too high, and in any case I could not bring him £10,000 in notes. He suggested that he would give us the antiquities and we could send the money subsequently, then he would send the photographs. In fact, he would prefer to keep the prints and send us the negatives. That would be fine by us. Of course I should have asked him to bring the negatives along for us to see, but I didn't, and I was kicking myself for the lost opportunity.

On the Thursday lunchtime Peter Clayton phoned, but I was not in my room. He left a message asking me to phone back. He was aware that I was going to Salisbury with Stuart the following day. He must have heard from 'John', who presumably rang him to confirm my story. Peter, of course, knew nothing of the police involvement, but he did know that my cover story was genuine. I could not phone him back because I did not want to be forced to lie to him. A message was passed on and Peter said that he would phone me at home. Fortunately he didn't, but waiting for his call gave me an uneasy evening.

On the Friday morning (22 October) Stuart and I had to meet the police at the Museum at 7.30, which meant a very early start for me. I got a taxi from Kings Cross, and they were already there in the forecourt — Jack Woods with DS Alan Wilson as the driver. We drove down to Salisbury and went to the Police Station, where we met the rest of the team — two cars had come down from Holborn (with four or five detectives); there were two officers from the Antiques Squad (including Tony Russell); and two from Wiltshire CID.

In the middle of the morning four of us (the DCI, a DS, Stuart and I) went into town to locate the Red Lion **(Colour plate 8)**. I lost my bearings as we went round the one-way streets, but we had a map and parked in a nearby street. I went out first and got a nasty shock as I went into the yard, because I couldn't recognise anything. Surely there couldn't be two Red Lions? Then I realised that I had approached by the back entrance. There were two yards meeting at right-angles, with entrances on two different streets. I walked in and had a quick look into the two bars, just in case 'John' was around. Then I went back and collected Jack Woods, who gave it the once-over and checked all the exits. We went back to the Police Station, and found that other detectives had already been round to identify the homes of Garriock and Rossiter — they had also been checking to see if either of them had had any previous form. We had set up headquarters in a corner of the police restaurant, where Jack Woods briefed everyone on the story so far — he called it a classic piece of detection — and outlined his plan. It was impressive to see the DCI in action, fully in command of the situation but listening to the ideas and objections of all. I couldn't have wished to be with a better team. Even Stuart and I put our oars in and made modifications to the overall plan.

Soon after 1 o'clock the detectives left to take up positions in the town. Trying to cover all eventualities, they had three cars stationed in the town centre, in private car-parks, in an attempt to counter the one-way system. It was possible that 'John' would do a runner, or he might want to take us elsewhere to look at finds or photographs, or even to visit the site. The DCI was keen that we should give him every opportunity to reveal the site. Stuart and I waited at the Police Station, where we had ordered a taxi for 2.10 to take us to the Red Lion. Originally we had thought of walking into town from the Railway Station, as if we had just arrived from London, but the road in was from the direction of 'John's' home, and it was just possible that we might meet him en route. Then there would be little point in walking all the way down to the Red Lion. So we fixed the taxi for a time that would coincide with the arrival of a train from London, and went from the Police Station direct to the Red Lion. We paid off the taxi and went in, watched, though we could not see them, by Jack Woods and two of his colleagues, who were stationed in a bar opposite. We went into the Reception area, rather early, and looking into the coffee bar on the left I noted a DS, Rick Player, reading his newspaper. To the right, in the small licensed bar, Tony Russell was sitting at a table facing me. Neither of them gave a hint of recognition. We wondered about selecting a seat, but the corner where 'John' and I had met before was already occupied, so we decided to hang around in the Reception, admiring a magnificent Grandfather Clock. 'John' arrived, also early, and he spotted us as soon as he walked through the door. He smiled, he was confident and trusting, and my heart sank, but there was no going back now.

I introduced Stuart, and 'John' asked if we wanted a beer or a coffee. We were happy with whatever he wanted, after all we had a man with a radio in each bar. He chose the coffee bar, perhaps because there was more space there, and led us right in to the room, beyond Rick, selecting a windowed alcove backing on to the yard. An alcove I had not spotted before, and the one position in the room that was behind Rick's back. From our point of view he couldn't have chosen a worse position. With some nifty footwork Stuart tried to retrieve the situation by going in first, along the bench into the very corner. I stood back to let 'John' follow him, and then I sat in a chair facing them, and as far out into the room as I could reasonably put it. Rick could just about see me, and that was vital.

As on our previous meeting in that room, 'John' wanted to start by seeing what we had brought with us. I set out the Museum photographs of McAlpine's 'Gloucestershire' hoard, the ones we had taken when we had borrowed the antiquities from Nicholas Wright. 'John' ordered coffee. He looked carefully through the photographs and declared that the artefacts were certainly from his hoard. Then he produced his own photographs, which he had brought, as before, in a white plastic carrier-bag **(Colour plate 9)**. Stuart had never seen them, and despite knowing the numbers of artefacts involved he was obviously stunned by this display. We had no difficulty in enthusing, and asking questions. Stuart eventually put the key question: it was so important, we just had to know where it had come from, surely 'John' could tell us? No, he was adamant, but perhaps when the dust settled, say in a year's time, he might be able to reveal the site. Then he referred to an artefact that I had queried on a previous occasion. I was not quite sure which one he meant, but apparently I had been worried that it was not on any of his photographs. 'John' had checked his negatives and had realised that one of them had not been printed, and this artefact was on the unprinted negative. He had all the negatives with him. I couldn't believe my luck. He brought them out (I could see the socks full of artefacts also in the bag) selected the relevant negative and passed it across to me. I held it up to the light, said that I couldn't see a thing because my spectacles were filthy, so I handed it across to Stuart, leant back in my chair and started to polish my spectacles.

That was the signal. 'John', oblivious, was beginning to show the antiquities to Stuart. It seemed to take quite a long time, and I could not be sure that Rick had seen me; afterwards Jack Woods expressed his amazement — 'He was still polishing those bloody glasses when we all walked in'. He pushed past me, and put his hand on 'John's' shoulder. Only then did 'John' realise that something was amiss. 'I'm sorry, John, but I am arresting you for being in possession of stolen property.' We were surrounded by detectives, the handcuffs went on. 'John' said 'Oh, no, not the handcuffs.' I couldn't look at him. They all went out, leaving Stuart and me. The Red Lion was functioning as normal, no-one seemed to have turned a hair, perhaps this was an everyday occurrence. We drank our coffee, and then I made a telephone call to Ian Longworth to put the Museum in the picture.

Afterwards we learnt that they had taken 'John' off and searched his car, which had been parked some distance away. Then they took him off to the Police Station, but he had nothing to say other than that he was a dealer and the antiquities were his. He obviously resented being handcuffed, which may have provoked his silence, but the police had not been prepared to take a chance on it. They were in a strange town, and 'John' was on his home territory; one of them related that the only occasion on which he had arrested someone without using handcuffs the prisoner had hit another policemen. Having settled 'John', the police then went round to arrest Rossiter, who was in bed.

Shortly afterwards Tony Russell appeared at the Red Lion, and said 'Well, Ian, do you want to see the site?' Rossiter had been very happy to talk: it was hard to appreciate our luck. We went in three cars to Netherhampton, just outside Salisbury, up a narrow lane off a main road, over a barbed wire fence into a field where a winter cereal crop was just starting to appear. Half way across the field Terry Rossiter stopped and turned to me 'Between you and me', he said, and then laughed as he looked round the assembled company. There was no place for confidences now. He might have wanted to spill the beans on previous occasions. After all, he had made the approach to Clare. But 'John' was the dominant character and had taken the lead. Towards the far side of the field, 32 paces in from a large beech tree, Rossiter stopped and marked the site. It was just below the crest of the field. He said that he had been metal detecting down the slope, further to the north, looking for Roman coins, and indeed he had found a coin. 'John' was higher up the field at the point indicated, when he found a bronze spear-head, and then got a much louder reaction. Rossiter indicated the size of the pit when excavated, about 2ft diameter and 2ft deep, smaller than 'John' had suggested. There was no earth in it, it was full of bronze artefacts.

Led by Terry Rossiter we then went off to find the landowner, a Mr Cook, a very old man who lived at Bemerton Farm. The buildings there were odd, and we could not understand the architecture, but subsequently learnt that it was the 'Russian Farm', built by an Earl of Pembroke for his mother, who was a Russian (another tale said that a Russian countess was the architect). It was part of the Wilton Estate, according to a notice at the side of the track. We parked on the track, and four of us went up the apparently disused front path and knocked on a door that looked as if it was seldom opened. At first it seemed that it was not going to be opened now, and we started to look for an alternative entrance, but there was a movement inside, the door opened, and a poodle shot out. Mr Cook stood in the doorway looking at us. He was indeed very old, 90, or so they said, but he was as bright as a button with good sight, good hearing and not at all gaga. Obviously he was surprised to find officers from the Police and British Museum on his door-step, but he coped well. He agreed that he owned the field, in partnership with his daughter, who came downstairs while we were talking. We went into the hall, and then into a dining or sitting room with a large table in the centre, and we tried to explain ourselves. Cook's daughter seemed to have more difficulty than he had in taking it all in, and she kept saying, 'This isn't really happening!' Having outlined the story, and shown them some photographs we arranged for a local policeman to take a statement in due course. We exchanged names and addresses and they said that in principle they would have no objection to the work that we then wanted to do: a survey and very limited excavation in order to identify the pit from which the hoard had been taken. We, as archaeologists, needed to confirm the source of the hoard, so did the police before they could bring their charges of theft, and obviously the landowners needed that evidence to stake their claim to the find.

We left Bemerton Farm and made our way back to the Police Station, where we had to kick our heels for quite a long time in the canteen. Meanwhile, 'John' was being interviewed in the presence of the duty solicitor. He stuck to his story that he was a dealer and did not know where the artefacts and photographs had come from. The police searched his house and brought back quite a lot of antiquities, most of them typical metal detectorist finds of little interest and no real value. He had quite a lot of coins at home, in cabinets, but the police rightly thought that they were not relevant to the present enquiry. Stuart and I went down into the cells and checked over the seized antiquities, confirming that there was nothing likely to be from the Salisbury Hoard. There was one Roman brooch that we could have found a home for. They had also seized his diaries for 1985 and 1986, but again there was nothing of real interest, though several entries referred to metal detecting. One entry (I think it was for 23 February) referred to one coin and beside it was a star of David. We did wonder if that was a symbol referring to the discovery of the hoard.

While we were waiting for the statements to be completed several of the detectives went off to phone their wives to say that they would be late back. They were quite sheepish and teased one another about it, and it was obviously one of the trials of the job. Sheelagh was well aware that I would be late, and there was no point in ringing her until I was nearer home. But I took the opportunity to phone Clare Conybeare, to tell her in particular that Rossiter had been arrested. He had mentioned her name when we were walking across the site. I also tried to phone Peter Clayton, but had to leave a message on his answerphone. Stuart went back by train, to Godalming, and I waited until Jack Woods had finished and got a lift back to Kings Cross, where I tried again to ring Peter but his line was engaged. When I eventually got home I found that he had rung Sheelagh in response to my message, but by that time it was too late to phone back, and he had said that he would be out all day on the Saturday.

I phoned Peter Clayton on Saturday evening. His wife said that he had just got in from a very long day, but he would like to talk to me later. When I phoned back he sounded flat, which was most unusual. Either he was depressed or perhaps just tired after the long day. He did not sound too surprised by my news, and I wondered if he had already heard from 'John'. I told him the full story, and he did not seem to bear me any animosity: towards the end he cheered up a bit and advised me to borrow the negatives from the police so that we could get a full set of prints. There spoke the archaeologist, and typical Peter, looking for a bright side and seeking to rescue something from the wreckage.

On the Monday morning, back at the Museum, I tried to see the Director, but he was busy during the day and could not fit me in until 5 o'clock. David Keys phoned about the middle of the morning. He knew already that two men had been arrested on the Friday, he knew that I was involved, and he knew that the site was near the Salisbury golf-course. He would not reveal his source, but it was not one of my contacts because I had not mentioned the golf-course to anyone (it was indeed next to the golf-course). At the time I thought that 'John' — it was difficult to think of him as Jim — might have contacted him, but in a subsequent conversation David was adamant that he had another source.

I wrote a long letter to the landowner, so that he would have some form of official document, and confirmed that we wanted to excavate the site as soon as possible. In the afternoon Jack Woods and Peter Basnett visited, hoping to catch up with a colleague who had set off to bring me the exhibits, seized photographs and antiquities. They wanted to retrieve one set of photographs because Basnett was going to see Cummings the following day and he was not familiar with the artefacts. At the same time Woods was going to see Martin. They sat in my room waiting for their colleague, and while they were there the telephone rang. It was Rose Anderson, McAlpine's assistant, who said that she had spoken to McAlpine and he was willing to sell us his 'Gloucestershire' hoard for £3700 which he would make up to his original asking price of £5000 by giving us a grant. My friends across the table listened with some amusement. I explained to Rose that there had been a change in the situation. The man she knew as John of Salisbury had been arrested. 'Arrested! By whom?' 'By the police.'

'Does that mean that you are no longer interested in buying the hoard?' I explained that the police would no doubt be calling in to see her, and suggested that she should keep the hoard intact until they arrived.

At 5 o'clock I went to see the Director (Robert Anderson had now succeeded David Wilson) with Fran Dunkels from the Press Office. I had kept the Press Office in touch with earlier developments because of David Keys' involvement, so Fran knew something of the background, but rather than tell the whole story twice I thought that it would be better for her to sit in on the meeting with the Director. He had had a busy day, looked tired, and was moving on to a further engagement so we did not have long with him. He listened to the story fairly impassively but he was sufficiently impressed to suggest that we should reserve the film rights! He was concerned that we might have made a mistake in buying the miniature shields from McAlpine. But if we had not bought them we would never have established their provenance and never appreciated the significance of the Salisbury Hoard. However, we had no time to discuss the matter further. I only just remembered to ask permission to carry out the excavation.

The following day, in the afternoon, Peter Clayton phoned to say that C. J. Martin had contacted him. Two police officers had visited Martin and had taken away the axe that Peter had been trying to borrow on our behalf. Jim Garriock had spoken to him, and was particularly resentful about the handcuffs; David Miller was furious. Peter was expecting a visit from the police, who might want to examine Seaby's books to see where the artefacts had gone.

On the Tuesday and the Wednesday I had numerous calls from David Keys checking the story that he was at last allowed to publish in *The Independent*, but my main task was making arrangements for the excavation.

4. The Excavation

There was only a week to organise the excavation: normally we had months. After setting the archaeological targets, the first stage in planning any excavation is to raise the money. In the Museum, excavation projects and their finances are controlled by the Trustees' Excavation and Fieldwork Committee which allocates funds in the spring. This works well because most excavations in England take place in the summer or early autumn, after the harvest. A last-minute project creates problems, but fortunately the Salisbury Hoard fell within the terms of reference of a project to which funds had already been assigned and, even more fortunately, by chance there was money in hand. After three seasons digging the site of the gold hoards at Snettisham (1990–2) we had attempted to solve some of the problems there by extending the project to cover Iron Age hoards in general. In 1993 we had investigated two other sites where gold torques had been found, and one of them had had a premature and very unsatisfactory ending. Having agreed to the project and accepted the implications of our archaic Treasure Trove laws (p. 150), the owner of this site had spoken to his solicitor at the eleventh hour and decided to vary his terms. In the week before the excavation was due to start he declared that he would not allow an excavation unless we agreed to pay him half the value of any discoveries. Finds from excavations are never purchased by any museum in Britain, they are always acquired as a gift. Excavations are costly, and archaeological funds are limited. Beyond that, if we found gold it might well be declared Treasure Trove, so it would belong not to the landowner but to the Crown. We could not pay the landowner for something that did not belong to him. There was no time for prolonged negotiations, but we went into the field in an attempt to change the farmer's mind. We failed, and packed up after a few days. Hence we were in the unusual position of having finance in hand, finance that had already been assigned to a project investigating Iron Age hoards. The Keeper recommended that it should be transferred to the Salisbury Hoard site at Netherhampton, and the Chairman of the Excavation and Fieldwork Committee, Sir Matthew Farrer, gave his approval.

The next stage was raising a team, and I had been making preparations over the past few days. The Museum does not have a permanent team of excavators because excavations are only an occasional feature of our lives. In our Department we organise no more than two or three each year, and they rarely last for more than a month. Usually two, perhaps three, members of permanent staff would go on the excavation and temporary staff would be recruited just for the month. All fieldworkers have the nucleus of a team, their own contacts, and mine went back more than 30 years. Sheelagh started her archaeological life as a Site Supervisor before becoming a specialist in human bones when we were digging major cemeteries in the 1970s and 1980s. On the smaller excavations of recent years she has taken charge of all finds in the field. Tony Pacitto worked with me on the first dig I ever directed, in 1956, and had missed very few since then; I would not have liked to go into the field without him. On this excavation his experience of detecting devices would be invaluable. For the younger element we had two members of permanent staff, Tony Spence, a Senior Museum Assistant, an experienced archae-ologist especially skilled at surveying and computer work; and Dave Webb, a Senior Photographer, excellent at his job but also a meticulous excavator, an archaeologist manqué. Dave's friend Ian Blomeley, a freelance archaeologist then employed as a despatch rider, could leave his job at a moment's notice to join us. Like Tony Spence and Dave Webb, Ian had been on every one of my digs for the past four years: a really useful all-rounder, and the owner of a Landrover. The five of them had been standing by for about a week, and had known that there might be something in the offing for a lot longer than that.

Other arrangements had to be made. In particular we needed to have huts and a loo, so I asked Andy Lawson, Director of Wessex Archaeology, to recommend a local Contractor. Andy also checked to see whether or not the site was a scheduled Ancient Monument: fortunately it was not, because that would have delayed us considerably. I needed to examine air photographs of the field. Normally that could have been done at leisure, but Mark Corney (Royal Commission on Historical Monuments) came to the rescue and agreed to sort out available cover and bring it out to the site. I arranged to meet both Mark and the Contractor on the Thursday afternoon. I phoned Paul Robinson to alert him to the excavation, and Stuart let Salisbury Museum know.

On the Wednesday Tony Pacitto came down and spent the night with us, and the following morning set off with Sheelagh and me in two vehicles. Ian Blomeley picked up Tony Spence in the Landrover and we arranged to rendez-vous for coffee at a Little Chef just outside Salisbury. There we reorganised, with Sheelagh and Ian setting off to sort out accommodation for us while the two Tonys and I went to see the landowner and organise the site. We arranged to meet up again for lunch at the pub at Netherhampton.

Mr Cook was at home with his daughter, Pam Lowrie, and her husband, who was a vicar. We sat down with them and I related the story again for the vicar's benefit, explaining our aims. Amongst the antiquities in the hoard were several socketed axes that looked silvery because of their high tin content: they had come straight from the moulds, untrimmed, and indeed the alloy made them so brittle that they could never have been used. One or two of them had shattered completely and there were many small fragments amongst the oddments in one of Jim Garriock's socks. It would have been quite impossible for the two finders to have recovered every tiny fragment and I was very confident that we would find enough to confirm the precise location of the pit. Other artefacts had also been broken, including some miniature shields, and with luck we might find a small part of one. I was keen to find fragments of both types in the same place, to confirm their association without a shadow of doubt. In the office we had checked some of Garriock's fragments with a small metal detector, the sort used in the home to detect nails in stud walls, and they had given good reactions. We told the landowner that we would first survey with the magnetometer to see if we could locate a pit; if successful we would dig by hand and carefully work through all its contents. With luck we might be finished within the week. But we had to have a base, a couple of mobile huts, within easy reach of the dig, and as there was a crop on the field we had to think carefully about access, to create as little damage as possible. We decided to meet on site immediately after lunch, to get this problem settled before Mark Corney and the Contractor arrived in the middle of the afternoon.

So we went off for lunch earlier than anticipated, and were finished when Sheelagh and Ian arrived. They had collected a list of accommodation, had checked out one place and were quite keen on a second that was quietly placed but a long way out of Salisbury: no real problem, because the last thing we wanted was to bump into one of the finders.

After lunch we met Mr Cook and the Lowries again. The field was completely surrounded with barbed wire, and we stopped on the track and looked over to the site on the far side; they did not want to walk across, there was little point in it. While we were standing there a couple of motor-cyclists roared up the track. Old Mr Cook set off towards them waving his stick and shouting. Obviously he could be quite aggressive when he wanted to be. We were told that motor-cyclists were a menace in the area, racing along all the tracks and even through the crops. There was a lot of vandalism and we would have to take great care to protect our tools and other belongings. There was a deserted farm at the far end of the field, and we went up to see if it would make a suitable base, but it seemed too far away, so the landowners agreed that we could put huts on the site itself. There was a track by the other side of the field, adjoining the site, but they said that it was gated, the gate was locked, and it was not on their land.

While the discussions were taking place, Tony Spence had made a start with the surveying. We re-located the pile of stones with which Stuart and I had marked the spot indicated by Terry Rossiter, and Tony then pegged a 20m grid for Tony Pacitto's magnetometer survey. Mark Corney arrived soon after the landowners departed, and the Contractor came about the same time. We dealt with the Contractor first, ordering two mobile huts, one to be an office doubling as a tool shed and the other to be a finds shed doubling as a mess. We had been given permission to remove the barbed wire from an entrance at the bottom of the field, but the track was too narrow to allow a low-loader to enter, so we would have to organise a tractor to pull the sheds into the field. That would be the best means of transporting the huts over the crop as well. Mark Corney had brought some air photographs and plottings, but although there were crop-marks in the vicinity there was nothing in our field.

Having given further thought to security I decided to phone the Museum and ask for a couple of warders to guard the site overnight. We had had a similar arrangement at Snettisham, when we were digging the hoards of gold, and it had worked very well. Before we left London I had spoken to Ken Wright, Head of Security, and warned him that I might need warders, so he was prepared. I had been thinking then about protecting any antiquities that we might have to leave in the ground overnight, but the warnings of vandalism and the prospect of a relatively high profile once David Keys' story broke suggested that added security was necessary. With the addition of warders to the team we had to order another hut for their base, and the Contractor couldn't supply beds so we would have to go out and buy some. That night Sheelagh and I and the two Tonys moved into our lodgings near Sixpenny Handley, 12 miles south-west of Netherhampton, and Ian returned in the Landrover to London.

The first two huts arrived the following day, Friday, which rather surprised us because they had not been promised before the Monday. I went round to Bemerton Farm and borrowed Mr Cook's man, Michael, and a tractor to drag them into position. The early arrival of the huts meant a slight change of plans for Ian, who had been intending to load up the Landrover with tools and take them, and Dave Webb, straight to Southampton where they were staying for the duration of the dig. Now they could bring the tools direct to Netherhampton, because we had somewhere to put them, and indeed we could use them over the week-end. Ian could also bring the alarm-post, which was too big for the warders' car. I phoned in and caught them before they set off.

So far we had approached the site across the field from the track that Terry Rossiter had shown us, but we now explored the nearer track. It was a hollow-way, quite deep in places, leading up the hill towards the Salisbury Racecourse, and was marked on the maps as a Roman road. As Mr Cook had said, it was gated and the gate was locked. On the far side of the hollow-way was the Salisbury golf course, so we went to the Clubhouse to make ourselves known and enquire about the locked gate. The Club Secretary was on holiday, but his assistant, a young girl, couldn't have been more helpful. The gate was unlocked to give us far easier access up a secluded tree-lined hollow-way, now rich in autumnal colours. The track had been gated to deter the motor-cyclists, but they gave us no trouble, although we did see them racing up and down on our original track. Despite being within easy reach of Salisbury, with a magnificent view of the Cathedral, we were quite secluded. Apart from invited visitors we saw only the occasional dog-walker and one or two golfers curious to investigate their new neighbours. We collected a surprising number of golf balls from our field.

Towards the end of the afternoon the two warders arrived. Graham and Eddy had both done shifts at Snettisham, and they settled in easily. We showed them where to get water at the Golf Club, but the more urgent concern was getting beds. The light was already failing when Sheelagh and Graham set off for Salisbury, but they returned

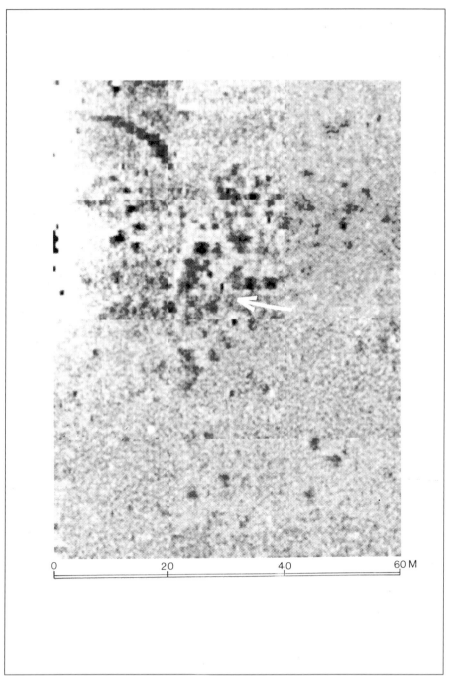

3   Plotting of the magnetomenter survey, by A L Pacitto. The dark
    markings indicate features cut into the chalk, especially a number of pits
    and the curved arc of a ditch. The white arrow indicates the place where
    the Salisbury Hoard had been buried.

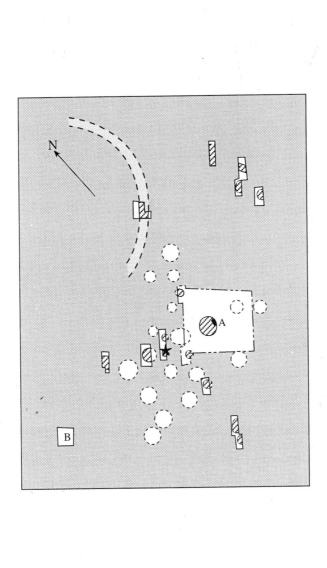

4   Plan of the trenches excavated at Netherhampton, to the same scale as
     the magnetometer survey **(Fig 3)**. Pits and ditches plotted by the
     magnetometer are indicated with dashed outlines; features confirmed by
     excavation are hatched. A = the site of the Salisbury Hoard; B = Hoard
     B; ★ = the site of the Salisbury Hoard as indicated by Rossiter.

successful and we left the site to the warders.

On the Saturday morning David Keys' report apeared in *The Independent* — a fairly large piece on page 3, illustrated with a photograph of the highly decorated miniature shield **(Colour plate 1)**. I spent most of the day organising the sheds, and Tony Pacitto made a start with the magnetometer survey. Over the weekend there were only the three of us, Sheelagh, Tony and me, because Tony Spence had gone home on the Friday, whilst Ian and Dave spent the weekend at Southampton, where Dave's wife worked at the University. On the Sunday Clare Conybeare came out, and we showed her the photographs of the hoard. Jack Woods had left us with one set of photographs and the negatives, which Dave Webb had printed up before he left London. He had brought a set of large-scale black-and-white prints to the site when he delivered the tools on the Friday.

On the Monday (1 November) Ian and Dave were back, and I sent Ian to the Railway Station to meet Tony Spence and then on to the Wessex Archaeology headquarters to collect a couple of trestle tables. By now Tony Pacitto had surveyed six 20m squares, some of them twice over. The easiest situation for us would have been to locate a single pit more or less where Terry Rossiter had indicated, with an area of blank chalk all around it. But that was asking too much. The magnetometer indicated a far more complex scenario. There seemed to be very many pits — up to 30 of them in one 20m square — and towards one side was the arc of a fairly substantial ditch **(Fig 3)**. We decided to start by confirming that the magnetometer anomalies really were pits, investigating a few by cutting sections. If we removed the plough-soil from half of a pit we should be able to see that half in plan as a darkish semi-circle cut into the chalk. Any pit that had been disturbed recently by the finders of the hoard would have a much darker filling and should be quite obvious. We started with an anomaly almost exactly where Rossiter had indicated; it was indeed a pit, a regular circle in plan, but it seemed undisturbed so we went on to the next one. By the Monday evening we had investigated six pits in this way, all seemed undisturbed and there was no point in removing more than about 10cm (4in) of earth below the level of the chalk **(Fig 4)**.

On the Tuesday Stuart came out in the afternoon and we had a visit from Peter Saunders and two of his colleagues from Salisbury Museum. The farm manager also visited: Mr Bright seemed to run several farms for different owners. Cook referred to him as the Farm Manager, but perhaps he was more of a contractor. When Stuart

1   *Decorated bronze miniature shield. Height 77mm (3in).*

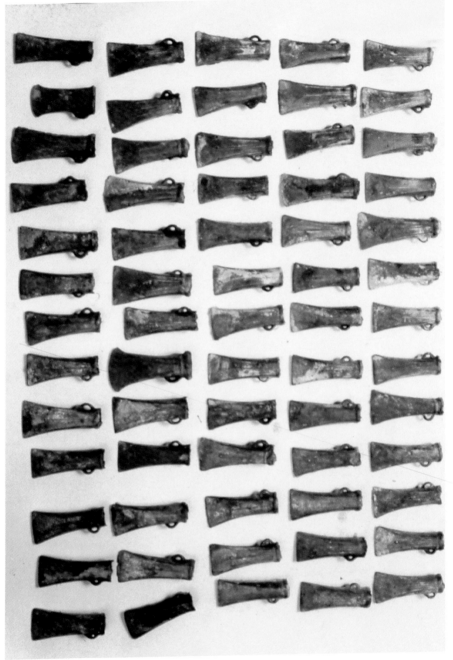

2   *Bronze socketed axes from the Salisbury Hoard, photographed by Brian Cavill soon after the discovery.*

*3   Bronze socketed axes, spearheads, daggers and gouges from the Salisbury Hoard,
photographed by Brian Cavill.*

4 *Bronze chisels, miniature cauldrons and other artefacts from the Salisbury Hoard, photographed by Brian Cavill*

5   *Bronze artefacts from the Salisbury Hoard, photographed by Brian Cavill.*

6   *Bronze artefacts from the 'Gloucestershire' Hoard.*

7   *Two joining fragments of a bronze miniature shield: the larger piece passed through several hands and twice crossed the Atlantic before being acquired by Devizes Museum; the smaller piece was retained by the finder. Height 71mm (2¾in).*

8   *The Red Lion, Salisbury.*

9   *Photographs, artefacts and packaging seized when Garriock was arrested.*

10   The re-discovery of the site of the Salisbury Hoard in 1994.

11   *The Drott stripping top-soil at Netherhampton.*

12   *The pit revealed in plan, before excavation. The dark patch on the right is where the Salisbury Hoard was found.*

13   *The pit in course of excavation.*

21   Roman bronze box with enamel ornament, from Elsenham. 46mm (1 ¾ in) high.

22 Snettisham: selection of artefacts from the hoard discovered by Charles Hodder in 1990.

23 Snettisham: hoard of gold torques, as excavated by the British Museum team in 1990.

politely asked the ninety-odd year-old Cook when he had retired, he responded sharply that he had not retired — 'Bright works for me'. Bright was a big jolly man, and most friendly. I explained our project, and said that it was now apparent that the site was so complex that we would want to return for a further season next year, whenever the field was free. The current crop would be harvested in July or August, and I asked what was planned for the following year. He said that he would settle for what suited us, and we agreed on peas, which meant that the field would be free from August to April. What a farmer! The archaeologist's dream. While I was dealing with the visitors the gang continued investigating pits in the same way; several more pits, as well as a stretch of the ditch, but no hint of recent disturbance.

One night we listened to a tape of the police interview with Rossiter to see if there were any archaeological clues. I was most impressed with the way in which Tony Russell had conducted the interview, very considerate and very much on the ball with archaeological as well as police matters. Rossiter came over as a thoroughly decent man who had fallen on hard times. He had lost his job through ill-health, had a broken marriage, and real financial problems. The temptation had been too much for him, and he had probably been influenced by Garriock. Garriock had found the hoard, and Rossiter had helped him to excavate it and had carried it away in the rucksack that he used for his metal detector when he was cycling, because he did not have a car. So much for the story that the hoard had been removed in a wheelbarrow.

They had taken the hoard to Garriock's house and washed it in water. Shortly afterwards Garriock had arranged for Brian Cavill, a fellow metal detectorist, to come over and photograph it. It had been laid out in drawers on the floor, and everything except the scrap had been photographed. The photographs seem to have been taken as a record of an incredible find, a keepsake, rather than a convenient way of touting the discovery around the dealers, as I had suspected. Garriock had contacted Cummings very soon afterwards, and he had come down and taken everything, even the scrap, apart from a selection — one of each type — retained by each of the finders. Cummings had paid £10,500, and that was shared equally between the two of them: there was no third party, as Garriock had told me. They had retained three of the shields, which Cummings had been very keen to acquire. He had been really persistent, and having started with an offer of £500 went up to £5000 before they eventually sold. Rossiter got £3000 of that, because he sold two of the three shields. Subsequently he had sold the rest of his selection, apart from the one miniature cauldron, to a dealer he had contacted via an advertisement in a metal detecting magazine. He had got about £1000 for them. There was another interesting detail. Rossiter had taken his children to the British Museum and in one of the galleries he noticed a collection of miniature shields. The label said that they were unique, and yet he had found some in the 'Salisbury Hoard'. He did not realise that he was looking at the shields that he had excavated.

By Wednesday it was apparent that we would have to change tactics. There were so many pits, and not a hint of recent disturbance. Perhaps Rossiter had mistaken the precise site. We were well into a field with no landmarks, and the spot he had indicated could have been several yards from the true position. Indeed it would have been amazing if he could have located accurately a feature that had been found more than eight years earlier. But I recalled that 'John' had said that they had visited the field in most subsequent years, which would have reinforced the precise spot in their minds. I phoned Jack Woods and asked if we could get Rossiter back on site, but he couldn't approach him now because Rossiter did not have a solicitor. So we decided to strip an area by machine and search the plough-soil with metal detectors as we had done at Snettisham and Essendon. If that was unsuccessful we would have to clean down to the chalk and examine the pits in more detail: it was beginning to look as if we could be here for some time.

I explained the problem to Mr Cook, who appreciated the need to get a result; it was the only way that we could prove that he was the owner of the hoard, and the only way that the police could bring a prosecution. Nonetheless he was muttering about compensation for loss of crop if we had machinery! Cook recommended a firm of contractors, so Tony Pacitto and I went off to see them, and managed to hire one of the very few Drotts in the area. They regarded the Drott as an antique and would have preferred to provide us with a digger and dumper truck, but the Drott was far more versatile for what we had in mind, and as for antique — well, we did come from the British Museum. The other move that we made was to boost the labour-force by recruiting Peter Makey. One of the mainstays of my team in recent years Peter was an excellent archaeologist, the hardest worker I had ever employed, and a constant source of amusement. He was an authority on flint tools and managed to find a surprising number of flints on all my Iron Age hoard sites. I had not contacted Peter at the start because he was working on a short-term contract for English Heritage, but he was based near Portsmouth and office-bound, so he jumped at the chance of having a weekend in the field.

The Drott arrived on Thursday morning, and we set it to work on a 20m square centred on the spot marked by Rossiter **(Colour plate 11)**. It started in the north-east corner of the square, stripping shallow spits of top-soil and dumping it towards the hedge. After each run we surveyed the new surface with two metal detectors, and by the middle of the morning we had found a tiny fragment from one of the 'tinned' socketed axes. Several more fragments appeared in the afternoon, all concentrated in the same area, and by mid-morning on the Friday we had identified the pit itself **(Colour plate 10)**. The Drott cleared the top-soil from an area around it and we thoroughly cleaned the chalk surface. We would never have found it with small trenches, because it was not what we had expected. We had been looking for a separate isolated pit, but our target proved to be a very small pit cut into the filling of a much larger pit **(Colour plate 12)**. The larger pit featured on the gradiometer survey, where it completely obscured the smaller one. Of the pits that we had investigated with trenches, we had consistently cleared the east half and left the plough-soil over the west half. Inevitably the key pit had been cut into the west half of the much larger pit.

We excavated the larger pit by cutting a section line through the centre — a line that also bisected the smaller pit — and then we removed the filling from one half. First we cleaned half of the later feature, the smaller pit, roughly rectangular in plan and only 65cm by 35cm (2ft 1½in by 1ft 2in) — amazingly small to have contained such a vast hoard. But there was no doubt that we had found the right spot because many more small fragments of bronze were recovered. The filling, as we had expected, was of relatively dark earth, mainly plough-soil put back by Garriock and Rossiter after they had removed the artefacts in February 1985. None of the original, Iron Age, filling survived. The bottom was less than 30cm (1ft) below the chalk surface: it would have been 50cm (1ft 8in) deep below the surface of the field. Having removed half of the filling of the smaller pit we then set about half of the larger pit, which was 2m diameter at the level of the chalk. It had not been disturbed by the metal detectorists and it might hold clues to the date when the hoard had been deposited. Either the hoard had been buried in the top of this large pit, as it had been filled, or perhaps more likely it had been buried later in a small pit cut into the larger one. If we had been able to excavate the original deposits we might have been able to resolve this point, but the metal detectorists had destroyed the evidence. However, as the larger pit was undisturbed, everything in its filling

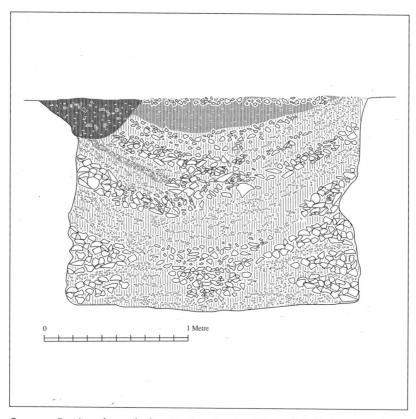

5   Section through the pit, showing its filling of chalk lumps and earth; the Salisbury Hoard was found in the small dark pit at the top left. Drawn by Karen Hughes.

was either contemporary with or earlier than the deposition of the hoard. The latest artefact from the hoard had been made no earlier than about 200 BC, we reckoned, and under normal circumstances one would have been happy to accept a date of about 200 BC for the deposition of the hoard. But this hoard covered an amazing length of time, with artefacts from almost every century from the 24th to the 2nd BC. It was quite conceivable that it had been buried in even later centuries. The dating of the larger pit could be crucial.

After work on the Friday I called round at Bemerton Farm to tell Mr Cook that we had identified the pit, and the following morning he and his daughter came out to look at it. Stuart was with us all that day, and Jack Woods visited, combining his visit with a couple of interviews in the area. We could get no more than two workers in the pit at any one time, usually only one, so we could not progress quickly **(Colour plate 13)**. Pete Makey worked as fast as any archaeologist could, but about 80cm (2ft 6in) down he discovered some articulated calf bones, which rather put the brakes on. They had to be cleaned, plotted and photographed. Dave Webb is a perfectionist, every bit of earth had to be removed from the bones before he would photograph them; then I plotted and moved them and Pete resumed work. The next delay was the discovery of pottery, first some large but very degraded sherds in the middle of the pit, and then a virtually complete pot at the bottom. It was Sunday afternoon before I could start drawing the section of the pit **(Fig 5)**.

Once we had located the hoard pit we had achieved our main aim, and had begun to look to the end of the dig. Everyone had interrupted normal life for the dig, and needed to know when it could be resumed. Our landlady wanted to know how long we were staying, and the warders would have to be relieved if we went on for a further week, but not if we stopped within a couple of days. Beyond that, there was a certain pressure from the weather, which was beginning to deteriorate: the long-term forecast was not good. When we had started on the large pit we had expected to finish work on the Monday and depart on the Tuesday, but by Sunday this plan was obviously too optimistic.

While the pit was being excavated and recorded, Tony Spence continued to survey the field and Tony Pacitto used the detecting devices. First he completed the magnetometer survey, and then he started with a deep-seeking metal detecting survey. Although we were trying to keep as quiet as possible about this project the precise site was known to several people and future publicity might well encourage the metal detecting night-hawks. There might well be another hoard in the vicinity, and it would be foolish to leave it and lose it. The machine we used was a relatively new acquisition which had yet prove its worth, doubtless because we had never used it over the site of a hoard. In theory it would ignore surface metal and small pieces in the plough-soil but detect more substantial deposits at a greater depth. Tony could work quickly with it, but because it had never located antiquities we had had no control, and I for one did not have too much confidence in it. However, this changed towards the end of Monday afternoon when Tony located a second hoard, about 17m away from the first. We investigated and discovered the rim of a circular bronze artefact, possibly a mirror. It was too late in the day to do any serious work so we covered it over and left the warders to guard it. I went round to Bemerton Farm to inform Mr Cook, and en route stopped at the telephone box to phone Ian Longworth.

On Tuesday it was raining so we erected a shelter over the new hoard. Peter Makey and Dave Webb continued in the large pit despite the rain, and found more articulated calf bones with the consequent delay. But we made good progress with the new hoard (Hoard B). The 'mirror' resolved itself into the broad flange of a short wide open-ended sheet bronze tube, beyond which was a narrow sheet-bronze collar and then, arranged in an arc, three cast-bronze collars. We had never seen anything like this, but their curved alignment and tapering diameters suggested that they had been fittings on a horn or something similar, whose organic components had long since disintegrated. Perhaps it had been a trumpet. Scattered in the vicinity were three other bronze artefacts, a spearhead, part of another, and a chisel **(Colour plate 14)**. Unlike the very much larger hoard found by Garriock and Rossiter, the new deposit was not compact, and we could not identify a pit: the bronzes seemed to be in the upper filling of a broad (and perhaps shallow) feature whose full investigation would have to await the next season here. Within the day we excavated, photographed, plotted and removed all but one of the bronzes: despite having warders on site it would have been unwise to leave anything *in situ*.

During the day Peter Saunders visited again, as did Clare and Nick Griffiths. Peter said that the local press was keen to know the precise site, but he had declined to tell them. There had been several news reports in the local papers, but no journalist had made a serious attempt to locate us. David Keys, who had announced our excavation in *The Independent* report, had said that the site was within 10 miles of Stonehenge. He wasn't trailing a red herring, rather he was trying to relate it to a well-known archaeological monument to give an approximate position to a general reader. But that diverted attention to the other side of Salisbury, and the suggestion that our hoard was religious led the press to the druids and strengthened the connection with Stonehenge. I was told that Jocelyn Stevens, Chairman of English Heritage, was worried that we might be disturbing his most famous site!

On the Wednesday we completed the recording of Hoard B, lifted the final artefact and carefully back-filled to prepare the way for re-opening next year. In the large pit the problem now was pottery: several substantial sherds from a much degraded pot that seemed to have been complete when deposited in the centre of the pit and had collapsed as it was back-filled. Then around the edge of the pit, in the sector that ended underneath Garriock's hoard of bronzes, we started to find other pots, more or less complete and certainly in better condition than the one in the middle. We spent a hard day excavating, photographing, plotting and then lifting the pots, and in the end we were left with an empty pit.

Thursday (11 November) was the last day of the excavation. Dave spent the morning cleaning up the large empty pit for a final photograph: 2m diameter and cut 1.4m into clean chalk, it looked quite impressive. The rest of us packed finds and belongings. Over the last few days pressure had intensified in the Pottery Shed as more and more finds had to be sorted, washed, dried, labelled and eventually packed. First thing in the morning we parcelled up the last of the finds, and by mid-morning the warders were able to set off to deliver tham to the Museum in London. I went round to the Golf Club to say good-bye to the Secretary; there was no need to see Mr Cook because he had been on site the previous day. We were ready to go at lunchtime, so leaving the Drott to back-fill the site we went down to the Netherhampton pub for lunch and then set off home. I took the Friday off work. On Friday evening I was lecturing to John Weeks' society at Foxton (p. 133), so we had finished just in time; earlier in the week it had looked as though I would have to cancel it.

5. The Collections

The week after the excavation, and well into the week after that, I spent as much time as I could checking the excavation finds. We had certainly found fragments from miniature shields and socketed axes, so we had confirmed the finders' overall story. But it would be even better if we could prove that we had found pieces that joined some of those recovered by Garriock and Rossiter. In the event I came up with only one positive join and it was not one that I had expected: amongst the excavation finds was a piece that fitted one of the curious 'ferrules' that Peter Day had sold us. That was particularly pleasing because we only had Day's word for it that they belonged to the hoard: they did not appear in Cavill's photographs. We had no reason to doubt Day's word, but here was the proof. I made no attempt to match the tiny fragments of socketed axes — that was a job for Stuart and as he had other commitments it would have to wait for another day.

I wrote to Mr Cook to clarify our position with regard to the ownership of the finds. Normally we would have asked the landowner to donate any finds before we started an excavation, but this Netherhampton project had been an odd one. Come what may, we had had to excavate to satisfy the police and ourselves about the precise location of the hoard. So in our only formal letter written before the excavation I had said that we intended to recover from dealers and collectors as many artefacts as possible from the Salisbury Hoard, and with the landowners cooperation we aimed to acquire them for the national collection. I had not mentioned finds from our own excavations. Now I drafted another letter, touching on the ownership of all the finds and the arrangements for the next excavation that we had already discussed in the field. Dealing first with the artefacts found by the metal detectorists, we would have to

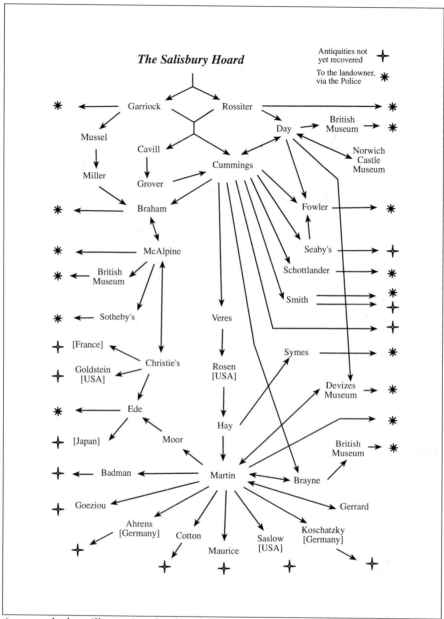

6   A chart illustrating the distribution routes of some of the artefacts from the Salisbury Hoard.

await a court case to disentangle the matter of ownership. If it was decided that Cook was the owner we would seek to acquire the miniature shields, the most valuable items in the hoard, for the same sum that we had paid McAlpine. Beyond that it was essential to acquire as much of the hoard as possible, to re-assemble it and keep it in the one place. With regard to the finds from our recent excavation, and I listed them, Cook was undoubtedly the owner, and I asked if he would be willing to make a gift of them to the British Museum. I raised the question of a further excavation, and asked if he would give us any finds from that.

In the Department we discussed the matter of publicity. So far we had restricted our comment to the information given to David Keys for his article in *The Independent* and to Andy Lawson for a brief piece in the *CBA News*. It was known that we had excavated and located the site of the hoard, but the precise location of the site and the nature of our finds had not been revealed. We decided to leave it at that pending the court case. In fact, over the next few months there was little press interest in the Salisbury Hoard, which was rather surprising because Fran had told me that during the excavation the Press Office had been bombarded by a local press determined to locate us and learn more about the operation. She had never known anything like it and had got the distinct impression that they would have been willing to bribe her!

While I had been on the excavation the police had been busy taking statements from dealers, and they had collected quite a number of antiquities **(Fig 6)**. We decided that it would be sensible to keep them at the Museum, partly because the police did not have storage facilities for antiquities but more importantly because we needed to correlate artefacts with Cavill's photographs. This was to be a long and painstaking task, because some of the types, especially the socketed axes and miniature cauldrons, included many very similar objects that had to be identified individually. Everything was packed in boxes, with sheets of polyethylene in which each artefact had its own shaped cut-out.

The first collection to arrive had been Garriock's, seized at Salisbury in the Red Lion. It now occupied two boxes, one with the reasonably complete pieces and the other with fragments. Most of McAlpine's 'Gloucestershire' hoard was also there. Four pieces from the published hoard had been dispersed, but we had been able to add four more from elsewhere in McAlpine's collection, recognised by comparison with Cavill's photographs.

The third main collection was more of a surprise. Peter Northover had told me that Robin Symes, the West End antiquities dealer, had some of the Salisbury Hoard, and I had passed the information on to Jack Woods. Symes was away at the time of our Netherhampton excavation, and we were told that his part of the Salisbury Hoard had already passed to a private collection, whose curator returned it so that it could be handed over to the police. The collection that we received included seven large flat axes that were obviously extraneous: quite different in style and in patina. But the rest, 84 items, seemed to be from the hoard, though they included several pieces that did not appear in Cavill's photographs. In particular, there was a surprising number of miniature cauldrons, 29 of them of which only four were in the photographs, but considering the rarity of the type surely they all belonged to the one hoard. Apart from two possible examples from our 'Batheaston' hoard all known miniature cauldrons came from the Salisbury Hoard.

Alongside the three major collections we had one box of individual items. There was Rossiter's miniature cauldron, the finest of the lot; a socketed axe retrieved from C. J. Martin (the one that Peter Clayton had attempted to borrow); and another, cleaned and sparkling, from Julia Schottlander. Apparently Cummings had sold much of the hoard to Maurice Braham in a transaction that had taken place in Schottlander's rooms, and this axe had been her commission.

When Jack Woods came in to take yet another statement from me, accounting for the excavation, he brought in another major collection, from the Scottish farmer, Smith. It had been held by the Museums of Scotland and Alison Sheridan had handed it over to Jack when she came down for a conference. Smith's collection had been purchased direct from Cummings.

Peter Day had written immediately after the excavation to say that he had read the press reports of our activities with mixed emotions, though he had been prepared for them by my letter on the eve of the excavation. Obviously he was pleased that the enquiries he had started had proved that the hoard was of great importance, but he was upset that the outcome was to be a prosecution. He said that he 'felt a certain empathy with one of the finders in that he was divorced shortly after the find and left without a job and with children to support. I feel he was an unwilling partner caught up in something beyond his control or comprehension. I shall be sad to see him further punished for his folly.' He thanked me for not revealing his identity to the police, but was puzzled by a message from the local police asking him to contact DCI Woods at Holborn regarding 'jewellery'. Jack Woods, who had indeed contacted him, though he had not received the address from me, said that Peter had been more than happy to talk about his involvement with the hoard. One fact that came out of their meeting was that, although Day knew Garriock, he had bought the antiquities from Cummings.

Jack Woods had learnt a lot more about the movement of the hoard, and he passed on the information. Some or all of the collection taken to Jonathan Rosen in the USA had been brought back by Malcolm Hay; he had sold most if it on to C. J. Martin, with some of the residue going to Robin Symes. Another dealer, James Ede, had phoned the police to say that he had two axes from the Christie's antiquities sale (lot 5, 27 April 1993): he sent one in, and said that he was trying to retrieve the other which had been sold to a Japanese collector. Jack Woods had spoken to Fowler who had acquired pieces from Seaby's and Cummings, but he had quite a collection of artefacts and was not sure which ones had come from the hoard. He was unwilling to relinquish all his rights, but would submit items for study.

In another transaction David Miller had bought a shield from someone called Mussel, who was acting for Garriock. He had paid £4200 for it at a fair, and had crossed the room to sell it for £5000 to Braham. Braham then sold a half share in it to McAlpine for £3000, and a half share in the other shields for £15,000.

C. J. Martin had provided the police with a complete list of his transactions with regard to the Salisbury Hoard, and Jack Woods sent a copy to me by fax. There were two lots that we could account for already, both sold to Devizes Museum. Otherwise, apart from two unsold axes now with the police, Martin's consignment had been dispersed. Some of it had gone back to Hay, and Jack Woods was dealing with that. Quite a few items, judging from the sum of money involved (£2350), had gone to a Mr Maurice whose address was unknown. Neither our Department nor Coins and Medals knew of a Mr Maurice who would fit the bill. As for the other names on the list, I wrote to each one and met with limited success. Two British dealers, John Moor, of Pocklington near York, and John Badman, of Glastonbury, had long since sold their pieces in the trade, which was hardly surprising. Moor's axe had been purchased by James Ede.

An English collector had bought 10 axes, but he phoned to say that this had been five years ago and they had now been sold and dispersed. Two of Martin's axes had gone to German dealer/collectors, who responded to say that they had been sold on at fairs in Frankfurt and Munich respectively, so there was no chance of identifying them now. An American dealer, Dr Arnold Saslow, had

bought two axes from Martin, and my letter to him provoked a
furious response. He was one of the largest coin dealers in the USA,
and had bought the axes at a fair at which he had probably spent
$10,000 — how could I expect him to know what he had purchased
from Martin! It would seem that American dealers do not have to
keep strict records, unlike their British counterparts, and one got the
impression that export licences were of little concern to someone as
important as Dr Saslow. Another collector or dealer who bought
from Martin lived in Jersey, but I got no reply to my letter and no joy
from subsequent attempts to track him down.

The last item in the consignment that Martin had purchased from
Rosen was a lot put into a Christie's auction: a chisel, gouge, punch
and dagger, lot no 83 on 4 May 1990. I wrote to Christie's and got the
expected response; they had a duty of confidentiality to their
purchasers unless they received a police request for information. Jack
Woods obliged, and Christie's promptly revealed that the purchaser
was Barbara Goldstein, of Salt Lake City. Mrs Goldstein was puzzled
by my enquiry, but confirmed that she still had the artefacts. I gave
her a brief outline of the problem, and as we already had good
photographs of her artefacts I suggested that she should keep them
and not dispose of them until we had sorted out the matter of title.

Apart from his acquisition from Malcolm Hay, Martin had also
purchased four axes from McAlpine, in 1991. Two of them had been
sold to English collectors in the last few months. Both responded to
my letters, and I advised them to return the axes to Martin and ask
for a re-fund. In due course they were handed in to the police. One
of these collectors came into the Museum about another matter, so I
showed him the photographs and some of the artefacts. He had heard
several rumours about the Salisbury Hoard and said that he had
recently sold a chisel from it: a distinctive piece with a particularly
long tang, he recognised it in one of Cavill's photographs. Later he
managed to recover it and sent it in to the Museum.

I made further progress with Martin's part of the collection when
I eventually located some of his lists. Quite a few of the antiquities
dealers issue lists, but we do not take all of them regularly at the
British Museum. However, other archaeologists and museum
curators had received lists, so it was a matter of seeing if any had kept
them. The most obvious contact came up trumps, Paul Robinson.
He seems to have taken Martin's lists for some years, and he looked
through them to see if there were any entries relevant to the Salisbury
Hoard. The earliest one that he found, March 1988, included seven
consecutive items ranging from a 'tinned' socketed axe (£185) to a

nail-headed pin (£30): the Salisbury Hoard was not mentioned. In May/June 1988 among 'special offers' were some 'British Bronze Age votive axe heads, from a bronzeworkers hoard found in the West Country ... Approx. 10cm in length and with a very pleasing silvery appearance. Perfect condition @ £185.00 each.' This item was repeated in the next issue, with the addition of 'other artefacts found within the same group, bronze chisels and gouges @ £110.00 each, bronze pins with slightly decorative heads @ £45.00 each'. The same items were still available in April/May 1989, with the note that 'the availability of bronze age material is always limited and our range is now coming to an end'; by now the 'tinned' axes were £200 each. They were still available in January 1990, but the next reference that Paul had located, June/July 1992, had a different selection. Item A67 was a chisel 'from the bronzeworkers hoard found in the Wiltshire region in the 1980s', and A68 a 'tinned' socketed axe 'from the same provenance and ex. Lord McAlpine of West Green'. The two were still available in November/December 1992, and the axe was the one on the proof list that Andrew Burnett showed me in October 1993 - the reference back on that list being to the chisel that had since been sold.

The only copies of Cummings' lists that I managed to track down were with Jeffrey May, at Nottingham. He did not have a complete set, but he checked what he had without finding a reference to the Salisbury Hoard. Jeffrey told me a horror story about a presumed temple site in Lincolnshire, a site that had produced miniature shields. The site had been found by a local metal detectorist, who foolishly told one of the dealers. Within weeks it had been ransacked, and the dealer was selling the artefacts, several of which Jeffrey had seen and recorded. Like Paul Robinson, Jeffrey is as much a numismatist as an archaeologist, and he has useful contacts in the metal detecting world. He receives information in confidence, is able to record artefacts and acquires a lot of useful information, especially about coins. But when information is obtained in this way contexts and provenances are unknown, or if they are known they cannot be published, so scholarship is the loser. The Lincolnshire temple site, if the miniature shields did indeed come from a temple, will never feature in an archaeological textbook. It is a moot point whether it is better to get a little information rather than to risk losing everything when contacts dry up. I sympathise very much with the predicament. Other numismatists faced with the same problems have managed to reconstruct, on paper, considerable parts of coin hoards by co-operating with metal detectorists, collectors and dealers. The information about these hoards is of similar quality to that available about hoards dispersed in the nineteenth century — some of it of great importance. Perhaps that is better than nothing but it is a very sad reflection on the state of British Archaeology.

John Fowler came up to London in January 1994 with a bag of antiquities. Another 22 pieces were added to the total. But we had photographs of most of them, provided by Peter Day some time ago, so there were no real surprises. Fowler, a property developer, arrived with his wife about 12.15 and they did not leave until 2 o'clock. He had tremendous enthusiasm, a very real interest in antiquities, and was a great talker. Stuart and I examined his collection and compared it with photographs that Fowler had brought, which showed that he had forgotten to pack a couple of the items. Some he had purchased direct from Cummings, others from Seaby's and perhaps from Peter Day as well. He was particularly concerned about the purchases from Seaby's because they had been cash transactions: occasionally he came up to London auctions with cash, and if he had any left he would call in and look at Seaby's stock. Sometimes he advertised for antiquities, and was contacted direct by metal detectorists. He was interested in provenance and several of his antiquities had been recorded at the British Museum. Some of his Salisbury Hoard pieces had been submitted to Exeter Museum, which we already knew from Andrew Lawson's records. Fowler had been advised by his solicitor that he had a valid claim to these antiquities, and he would put it in jeopardy if he handed them over to the British Museum. He was anxious that the Museum would not do a deal with the farmer behind his back, and very much wanted to retain at least some of the pieces. He would not mind us keeping the more unusual ones, but he would like, say, one or two of the axes. We showed him everything we had from the hoard, and all the photographs, and he left us with a copy of a letter he had written to Jack Woods.

Jack Woods had been preparing the case with the Crown Prosecution Service and wanted me to make a further statement — my third — to satisfy them that the find was not Treasure Trove, and to give our estimated minimum valuation of it at the time of discovery. Stuart and I sat down to it and worked out an approximate valuation — at least £80,000, of which the miniature shields accounted for £50,000. Over the past few weeks Stuart had spent a long time checking my correlations and adding more of his own, because I had not attempted to sort out the axes. When he had finished Tony Spence set up a database recording all the correlations, which were looking quite complicated now. Stuart had ended by comparing the hoard items with the excavation finds and had found no fewer than five joining pieces between the two groups — all axe fragments — to add to the one join that I had recognised **(Colour plate 15)**. This critical piece of information, too, was added to the statement.

In the middle of January 1994 it was announced in the press that McAlpine was selling his Cabinet of Curiosities, which seems to be his own description of his dealing collection. Both *The Times* and the *Evening Standard* devoted a full page to it, with colour photographs. They were intrigued by the list of items for sale, including a mummified puffer fish, skeleton of a panther, a stuffed lamb with eight legs, a Nootka wooden mask, and African necklaces. Apparently McAlpine had started collecting at the age of six, formed a huge collection of policemen's truncheons and progressed to modern art and early Scottish weapons. 'I simply like things that have an innate beauty .... You have to imagine the part these things have played in people's lives, their part in history', was one of the quotes. The articles concentrated on the eccentric collector rather than the dealer, though he did say 'This is just stock. I was dealing in these items in this gallery and I want to move to a smaller place. There is far too much here. I would rather deal in, say, ten pieces. Ten expensive pieces.' In *The Independent* he added that his decision to sell was influenced by the illness of a partner (presumably Braham), and the fact that 'the level of business has fallen right off in the last two years'. The sale was scheduled for Sotheby's and it was estimated that it would raise about £200,000. *The Independent* mentioned that it came four years after he had sold the contents of his former home, West Green, for £1.5 million. *The Times* included references to the antiquities trade, and especially to the Salisbury hoard:

> The field of antiquities is notorious for illegal excavations and smuggling [wrote Sarah Jane Checkland, their saleroom correspondent] and sellers often do not know, or care, to reveal where they got them from. As a result most sale catalogue entries are limited to descriptions of the objects, with no provenances. The McAlpine collection will be no exception. To minimise the risk of acquiring pieces of questionable origin, he avoided buying through 'runners' (opportunist small-time dealers who scour the provinces for treasures then rush them to London to make a fast buck) and instead, used a coterie of trusted dealers, who would ring whenever they encountered anything up his

street. 'Once you've got a name for wanting something, it appears,' he says. This does not mean he escaped official enquiry into the sources of certain objects. But, being made of stern stuff, he refused to be fazed, and relates incidents with relish. When the police arrived recently to seize about 30 Bronze Age objects, for example, they 'frightened the life out of my poor secretary' but, luckily, 'I was on holiday'. The items, allegedly found by two metal detector enthusiasts on Salisbury Plain and offered to Lord McAlpine by 'a man called John of Salisbury', are now sitting at the British Museum awaiting their fate.

The sale duly took place on 17 February, and raised more than expected, £300,000, doubtless because of the publicity. Curiously the catalogue was not circulated to subscribers. Peter Clayton phoned to say that he had gone round to collect one, and we had to send for one. Three of my colleagues went to the viewing, which was for much longer than usual. Stuart identified another of the Salisbury hoard gouges, which was consequently withdrawn. This prompted further police interest in McAlpine, who was interviewed by Jack Woods on 11 March, as reported the following day in the *Daily Mail*. Asked about his relationship with Braham, McAlpine had said that they were not in partnership, though they occasionally bought items together. Apparently he had not appreciated that I suspected that the hoard was stolen property. He told Jack that originally he had intended to help with negotiations with 'John', but when he realised that Seaby's were already handling them he decided not to bother.

We had now seen quite a number of pieces that seemed to belong to the hoard, and had been circulating with it, that did not appear in Cavill's photographs. Was it possible that Cavill had more photographs? I asked Dave Webb to have a good look at the negatives. By matching the cut edges and frame numbers he was able to show that at least three films had been used. They were shot in one session, possibly two, with the artefacts on a white card laid on a floor with a brown carpet. The photographer had used a tripod and probably a portable flash lighting kit. He had started with small groups of objects, moved on to individual objects and ended with large groups. Only the last three frames of the first film are present, so perhaps the film was already in the camera and half-used when the session started. The last three shots of the second film are missing, and the third film is represented by only three negatives — the first and fourth frames are missing, along with any frames subsequent to the fifth. So within the sequence there are five missing negatives, and there could be others before or after the sequence: were they blank (there could have been a problem synchronising the flash) or were other photographs taken? As they are not studio shots it would seem that Cavill took the photographs at Garriock's house, then developed and printed them himself (Dave did not think that the prints were the work of a commercial laboratory). Cavill had returned the 13 cut negatives to Garriock together with prints of only 12 of them, and Rossiter was provided with a duplicate set of the 12 prints. Whether or not other negatives were printed is unknown, but at least one of the 13 negatives had a third print taken from it, because Paul Robinson had acquired one from Cavill (though it could not have been obtained at a coin fair in November 1984 as we had been told originally); and Nick Griffiths thought that Cavill had some prints locked away.

Stuart went down to Devizes and spent about four hours recording 50 Salisbury Hoard items on display, and comparing them with our photographs; then he brought back about 90 items that were not on display, but all registered. They included two more 'ferrules' like those we had acquired from Peter Day, part of a miniature shield, and one or two oddities including a piece of sheet bronze that might have been a miniature currency bar. Among the artefacts that he recorded in Devizes was an axe that he thought was not bronze but copper. If so, it was the earliest artefact from the hoard, dating from about 2400 BC.

I needed to know more about Jonathan Rosen's part in the story; Martin had acquired a substantial number of antiquities from Rosen. My first move had been to write to Peter Northover, who first told me about Rosen's involvement, but that came to nothing so I decided to write direct. No response. Then I tried his assistant, Babcock. Still nothing. Next I sent copies of my letters to Rosen and Babcock across to John Curtis, Keeper of Western Asiatic Antiquities. Rosen was a 'Friend' of their Department, as well as being an 'American Friend' of the Museum. It took him quite a long time, but eventually he managed to speak to Jonathan Rosen in London. Rosen said that he had had the antiquities that I was interested in for about a year, round about 1986. He had no records of them; in fact, he realised that they needed cataloguing and as he had neither the time nor the inclination he decided to sell them — everything went to Malcolm Hay. Rosen had purchased them from Bill Veres, a Hungarian dealer living in London. Veres (who had already made a statement to the police) had bought them from Cummings.

In July Peter Day enquired about progress with the court case, and said that he understood that most of the hoard had now been traced. So I worked out some figures for him. Apart from the Devizes collection, which was complicated because we had yet to correlate all the fragments, we had details of 442 objects from the hoard, and had located 224 of them. So we were only half-way there. And of the 224 pieces located only 25 had been acquired and even their future was not secure because there was doubt about our title to them. The British Museum aimed to acquire legally all the pieces that could be located, but for that we would have to await the outcome of the trial.

6. The Trial

Garriock, Rossiter and Cummings appeared before the Clerkenwell Magistrates on Wednesday, 30 March 1994. I did not go, and got no first-hand account of the proceedings, but subsequently Nick Griffiths sent me a cutting from the *Salisbury Journal* (7 April) which may have been the only published account. The two Salisbury men were accused of stealing artefacts worth £83,000 from a site 'eight miles south of Stonehenge' and Cummings was charged with receiving stolen goods. The Crown prosecutor said that it was a very involved case and 'asked magistrate Mark Romer not to set a committal date for the trio, because police wanted to interview a fourth man "of some public standing" believed to be involved. All three were granted unconditional bail to reappear on April 27.'

But the fourth man, of some public standing, was not charged. The committal proceedings for the other three were postponed again and again and again — on several occasions the dates coincided with the rail strikes that ran throughout the summer of 1994: eventually they took place in October. During these seven months the police made various moves to strengthen the case, and took yet another statement from me, clarifying points from my earlier statements at the request of the CPS.

In July the police asked to borrow our official file on the Salisbury Hoard. All the evidence that would be produced by the prosecution had to be made available to defence solicitors, but in addition they had to be shown any 'unused material' that related to the case. Our file came into that category. I did not feel that I had the authority to release the file, and indeed before we were done we involved Ian Longworth, George Morris, the Director and the Treasury Solicitor. The Director ruled that we should make all relevant papers available to the police and to the defence solicitors.

Jack Woods and Richard Atkins (CPS) visited the Museum to check through our paperwork. Atkins explained the problem of disclosure of evidence, a development resulting from the trials of IRA terrorists. He needed to see our official file and any other papers that I had that might be relevant to the case. This included my unofficial files (scribbled notes, copies of official papers and various oddments), excavation note-books and plans. Apparently, as a public servant, I was in the same position as a police officer investigating the case. Everything that I had committed to paper, whether or not it had been seen by the police and the CPS, would have to be made available to the defence solicitors. The two of them looked through my papers, found nothing of interest, and asked if there was anything else. No. Then Jack raised the matter of my book — an early draft of the present text — which I must have mentioned to him. I could not believe that it could be regarded as evidence. It was entirely secondary, a factual account based on papers in the official file. Richard Atkins wanted to see it. They glanced through it and Atkins said that it was most important, and that we could have ended in trouble if it had not been declared. I was amazed. I ought to explain about this book, now being regarded as evidence. It started life as a series of file notes, developing as a diary. The story was complicated and there was a need to get all the facts recorded while I could remember them. Some of the file notes read like a detective story, and the ongoing tale was obviously fascinating to friends and colleagues. Its progress was given a boost when I went to a conference in Belgium in February 1994. I showed photographs of some of the artefacts to our Belgian colleagues, and they caused quite a stir. Shortly afterwards I had to do a presentation on the Salisbury Hoard to a group of Trustees. I tried to compress the complex story into about a quarter of an hour. They were impressed, and it was suggested that I should write a popular book about it. Thereafter the file notes and diary started to become a book.

In August Jack Woods went down to Salisbury and collected an artefact that had been there quite a long time, a miniature cauldron, handed in by a solicitor representing Mrs Rossiter. He also took another statement from Nick Griffiths, and visited Mrs Lowrie. Old Mr Cook had died earlier in the year, his 91st year, and his daughter had inherited the farm. Jack needed a death certificate for the old man, and permission to look at the farm's solicitor's papers, another matter of undisclosed evidence. He got the impression that Mrs Lowrie would be favourably disposed towards the shields staying at the British Museum. He spoke to Mr Bright, the farm manager, and was told of the possibility of housing or light industrial development in the vicinity. So perhaps the Netherhampton site would be threatened, which would open the door to large-scale excavation financed by English Heritage or a developer (and presumably carried out by Wessex Archaeology, because the British Museum would find it difficult to get involved in fieldwork on that scale).

In October a solicitor for one of the Salisbury defendants phoned to arrange a date to view the unused evidence. He was lucky to catch me in, my only day in the office between an excavation at Essendon and a holiday in Crete. I arranged for him to be shown the papers while I was away, but he was also keen to see the typescript of my book. That was impossible. One copy was at home (and as I was leaving at 7 o'clock in the morning I could not post it) and the only other was with the police or the CPS. In the event the CPS made a further copy for him.

The committal proceedings were to take place before a Stipendiary Magistrate at Wells Street Magistrates Court, and I had been told to present myself there as a witness on Tuesday and Wednesday, 25 and 26 October, at 9.45 am. The court-house was just north of Oxford Street and only about 10 or 15 minutes from the Museum. I arrived on time and was shown into a waiting room on the ground floor. Pam Lowrie was there already, with her husband and daughter for support. Our case was in Court 2, on the first floor, but they kept us downstairs in the ante-room to Court 1, presumably so that we would not have to mix with the defendants. After quite a long time Jack Woods looked in to say that he wasn't quite sure when we would be needed, and he came back about 11 o'clock to say that it looked as though they would be calling Mrs Lowrie only, but he wanted me to go with her to the ante-room upstairs (by then the defendants were in court). Mrs Lowrie spent about 10 minutes in court and then was told that she could go; I was not needed. Apparently the defence had been trying to claim that the late Mr Cook's evidence was not admissible. Hence there would be no proof that the metal detectorists were operating without permission. But the magistrate decided that Cook's statement was admissible. The evidence was then heard, via statements read out in court, but no witnesses were called. Later I was notified that the trial would take place on 24 April 1995, at Knightsbridge Crown Court.

Just before Christmas I wrote a letter to Mrs Lowrie to make provisional arrangements for an excavation after harvest in 1995, and another to the Contractor who had provided the Drott, to get estimates so that I could put in my bid to the Trustees Excavation and Fieldwork Committee. Towards the end of January the police came round to photograph the entire hoard. They had wanted everything in one shot, but they had to settle for three: with these photographs they hoped to avoid having to take the artefacts to court, though the judge and jury would probably want to see a sample.

On Monday, 24 April, I had to set off early, to get to the Museum and collect a box of antiquities needed by the court. DC Andy Cockburn arrived at 8.30 to take me and the box to Knightsbridge. I was surprised that we headed east, rather than west, and even more so when I was told that we were making for Blackfriars Bridge. Apparently the Knightsbridge Crown Court building was being refurbished, and as an interim measure they were sitting in a new court suite at Borough, Southwark.

I went to the Prosecution Witnesses Room, signed in, and was given an expenses form. Several others came in, and did likewise, and one of them seemed to show a particular interest in my box. It was then that I noticed that it was labelled on the outside, 'McAlpine antiquities'. When I was moved to another waiting room, the interested witness came with me, and we introduced ourselves. He was Brian Cavill, the photographer. I complimented him on the quality of his photographs of the Salisbury Hoard, and he told me that he had been given a small collection of artefacts as payment for taking them. The pieces that he acquired had been photographed on a blue background, whilst the main set had a white background. This turned out to be quite significant, because all the artefacts on the blue background had been recovered from McAlpine, who had bought most of them in a separate batch from Braham. There was one discrepancy, a very small axe in McAlpine's group did not appear in Cavill's photographs, where its place was taken by a more typical Salisbury Hoard axe. It seemed that there had been a muddle at McAlpine's, or at an intermediary dealer's. Stuart had already identified the very small axe as an East European artefact and a most unlikely element in the Salisbury Hoard. McAlpine/Braham had acquired Cavill's collection separately from another source, or at least via another route, but they knew that this second instalment was also part of the 'Gloucestershire' hoard because it was published as such in the Ashmolean's catalogue.

The photographs of Cavill's collection provided a further insight, because they included two miniature shields. But they had not been passed to McAlpine at the same time as the rest of Cavill's antiquities. It would seem that all the miniature shields were kept by Braham, and did not enter McAlpine's books until they were given the number M5519 on 7 June 1989, the day before they were entered as sold to the British Museum.

Meanwhile, back at the court, I chatted to Cavill for quite a while: he had lots of metal detecting stories. He was the Chairman of a metal detecting club, and had done work for archaeological units. He told me about his collection of buckles, of which he had been preparing a catalogue. The next witness to arrive was Mr Oglethorpe, Cook's solicitor (now retired) and executor; then the three Lowries and Clare Conybeare.

Jack Woods came in and chatted, followed by Richard Atkins. We were given our statements to read, because they had been taken months before, and we needed to refresh our memories. They were quite short, a single paragraph as far as I could see, apart from mine which went on for 17 pages. I read it through, and it seemed to be muddled, because of the sequence of the policeman's questions, and I would have liked to improve on the wording: but that's the way statements are taken.

Originally I had been told that I might be needed for up to a fortnight, so I had struck out two weeks in my diary, but the other witnesses there had been summoned for the one day only. About 11 o'clock Richard Atkins told us that there would be some delay. The case was starting with legal arguments and the judge had decided not to sit on the Monday afternoon, or on the Wednesday. The intercom then called another case to our court (Court 5); our witnesses were getting restless. Eventually we were called, and assembled outside the court, where we were told that on the Tuesday there would be legal arguments and the jury would be sworn in, but that witnesses would not be needed until Thursday, apart from Clare who was down for Friday. All the others seemed to have other commitments for the end of the week; the Lowries were moving house on the Thursday! I asked about Stuart, who had originally been told to be available on the Tuesday, and had had to alter plans and fly back from Italy. The Defence had now decided that Stuart would not be needed. He could have stayed in Italy. I left Jack Woods and Richard Atkins pacifying the other witnesses and made my way back to the Museum. At the end of the day there was a message from Holborn Police Station to the effect that I would not be needed until next week, and Stuart would also be needed. What confusion!

In the event Pam Lowrie gave her evidence on the Tuesday. The newspapers on the Wednesday gave considerable space to reporting Jonathan Laidler's opening address for the prosecution. Needless to say McAlpine's name got into all the headlines, with his photograph in both *The Guardian* and *Daily Mail*; *The Guardian* and *The Times* also had photographs of Garriock and Rossiter, and *The Guardian* added a photograph of Cummings in a piece that occupied half a page. At the end of the day I phoned Jack Woods to confirm that I would be needed on Thursday. He said that the legal arguments had gone our way, and they had all been raised by Rossiter's lawyers. They had tried and failed to claim that both Cook's evidence and the police interview with Rossiter were inadmissible.

On Thursday I arrived at court in good time and saw several photographers outside. As I approached they dashed forward to photograph a distinguished-looking gentleman emerging from a taxi. I slipped behind them and as I went in I heard the man say — 'No, not me' — he was in fact Cummings' solicitor. In the witness room was Mr Oglethorpe, along with Mr Bright (the farm manager) and Mr Hurly (one of his men). Bright related how one of the defendants had got into the same carriage of the train at Salisbury, sat opposite them (not knowing them) and chatted with a colleague, mentioning that they expected the trial to go into a third week. I took the opportunity to discuss dates for the forthcoming dig, and Bright said that the crop would definitely be off by 14 August. He also said that Meridian TV (the ITV station for the South) had shown an air photo indicating the precise site, the first time that it had been revealed, and he anticipated trouble. It had been the opening item in the regional news.

Oglethorpe went in first, was a lot longer than expected, and was followed by Bright and Hurly. Meanwhile Brian Cavill had arrived. He told me that he had remembered the precise date of the discovery: it was a Saturday afternoon, and the day before he had had a car crash: it was 23 February 1985, the date that had been starred in Garriock's diary. Cavill was called next, and about 12.30 I had to move from the waiting room to one of the seats in the corridor outside Court 5. But by 1 o'clock I was still there, and we went off to lunch in the same canteen as Garriock and Rossiter. Just before lunch a press photographer asked me to go outside for a photo, and then Meridian TV filmed me walking into the court building.

Cavill was still being cross-examined after lunch: all the witnesses had taken longer than I had expected and considering the length of their statements compared with mine I could see that I was in for a long haul. Later, when I gave my evidence, I realised that waiting for the judge (Judge Christopher Hordern) to take down notes of the evidence was one factor that slowed down the proceedings.

I think it was about 2.45 when I was called. From the witness box I faced the jury, with the judge to my right, a row of barristers to my left, then a row of solicitors, and behind them, slightly raised and beyond a low glass partition, the three defendants. The press and public were in five or six rows slightly behind me to the left. My examination in chief went quite well, though I got myself into a tangle trying to give a simple explanation of the significance of provenance. I was allowed to consult my file and taken through my statement and file notes in a good logical order. Jonathan Laidler, the prosecution barrister, led me, and I had to answer in my own words rather than read from the file.

Cross-examination started with Garriock's barrister who went through several details that seemed irrelevant. Treasure Trove, for instance. He was also concerned about the numbers of artefacts, and mentioned the artefacts still on display at Devizes Museum. He tried to trip me up on one or two points, but I saw them coming (afterwards Richard Atkins said that the cross-examination was pedestrian, so I hadn't been all that clever). 'You are fascinated by this case?' 'Yes.' 'So much so that you are writing a book about it.' 'We always publish the antiquities we find.' 'In a book?' 'I have written books, papers and notes: it depends on the importance of the find. This is a very important find.' I went on to point out that the book he was referring to was not the definitive report: some of the Trustees had suggested that I should write a popular account. The book was very much above-board. Following up the matter of Treasure Trove, he noted that I had said that the hoard was a votive offering. I elaborated, and said that there was probably a religious reason behind the assemblage of the artefacts, and certainly the latest of them were miniatures and would have been votive, but the precise reason for depositing the group was unknown. It could have been a votive offering, or they could have been buried for safe-keeping. He asked if I subscribed to the view that finders were keepers, and I said that with the exception of Treasure Trove all artefacts belonged to the owner of the land. He suggested that it would be different if they had been found on public land, and when I said that that would make no difference he thought that His Honour would have something to say about that. His Honour merely shrugged and looked disinterested. Garriock's barrister suggested that I would like to see all antiquities as the property of the state. I asked what had made him think that. He seemed rather taken aback, and said that he had been asking a question. The judge intervened to say that it was an irrelevant question, too. His Honour was getting tired of this line of questioning. At 4.30 the barrister looked towards the clock and the judge terminated the session.

Jack Woods had told me that I might be late back that night, and now I found out why. It was his leaving party and Richard Atkins took me round to a pub in Holborn where the party was well under way. I recognised several faces. Again I was greatly impressed with the team spirit that he had created. They all thought that he had been treated shabbily. It had been decided that CID at Holborn could be run by a DI instead of a DCI, so Jack had been moved to Internal Police Complaints. It seemed a waste of a first-class detective.

On Friday morning the court resumed shortly after 10.30, with me back in the witness box. Garriock's barrister had no further questions, so Rossiter's barrister took over. He too raised the matter of Treasure Trove, which didn't get us anywhere. Otherwise he was concerned to establish how cooperative Rossiter had been. Then it was Miss Smith, Cummings' barrister, who was expected to be more formidable than her colleagues. Before she got started there was a problem with unused evidence, and a break for about 20 minutes for it to be sorted out. Afterwards I was told that the unused evidence was a £300 bill that Mrs Lowrie had presented to the police (and they had paid) for loss of crop in the course of the 1993 excavation: it was the first that I had heard about that one.

Miss Smith cross-examined me for about an hour. She was particularly concerned about valuation, and was seeking to show that we had paid too much for the shields. She turned to the photographs and started to indicate the artefacts that Cummings had not handled, so I asked if there was a list of the artefacts that he had handled. 'Of course', she waved at her papers. (If such a list existed it could prove really useful, but the defence does not have to make unused papers available to the prosecution, so we shall never see it.) I think that she was aiming to get me to give valuations for individual items that Cummings had not handled, starting with the best-decorated shield. But the judge interrupted her and said that in this case valuation had very little relevance. She thanked him, and said that that would save a considerable amount of the court's time, putting a pile of papers to one side. She raised one further point on valuation: she suggested that I had told Veres that the Museum had paid too much for the shields. I had never spoken to Veres. She made the allegation again, and I was beginning to get annoyed. I had never met him and never even spoken to him on the telephone; I had never told him or anyone else that we had paid too much for the shields because I did not think that we had paid too much. We had paid a fair price.

She mentioned the three shields that Cummings had told me he still had at home. Surely I had realised that was a joke? It hadn't sounded like a joke to me, but my acquaintance with Cummings was short and I was not aware of his sense of humour. Cummings had told me that he bought the shields from a Salisbury coin dealer and (she had read the draft of my book) I had not believed him. I agreed that I had set off on the wrong track. But he was telling the truth? Yes. And if I had asked him who the dealer was, then he would have told me? He had not offered the information and I had not pursued the matter. (But I was quite sure that he would not have told me.) She referred to Cummings' catalogues and said that he had openly advertised antiquities from the Salisbury hoard. I had never seen one of Cummings' catalogues. That surprised her because she had a copy from one in her papers, supplied by the Prosecution who had obtained it from the British Museum. Now I was the one to be surprised. It turned out to be one of the photocopies provided by Andy Lawson, presumably obtained from Peter Day or Devizes Museum, but there was no indication that it had been issued by Cummings.

She turned to the matter of McAlpine's 'Gloucestershire' hoard that we had valued at £3100 and he had offered us for £5000. He had offered to make up the difference with a loan? No, not a loan but a grant. She also mentioned the three ferrules that we had bought from Peter Day for £15, despite the fact that they were not in the photographs. Yes, that had worried me, but when we excavated the site we found a joining fragment, proving that at least one of the ferrules had been in the hoard. Had Peter Day told me that he had bought antiquities from Rossiter. No, that was news to me. Leading up to the arrests, I got my word in about the sense of urgency created when 'John' had been advised to destroy the photographs and sell his antiquities in the trade, and McAlpine had attempted to sell his at Christie's. She finished with me soon after 12 o'clock, and I was then allowed to stay in court and observe the proceedings. The next witness was Peter Day.

I had not met Peter, though his correspondence with me had provided vital clues. He had come across the hoard first at a fair at the Cumberland Hotel (the day before a sale of gold nobles from the West Country — he had come up to view the nobles). He had toured the stalls asking if anyone had Bronze Age antiquities. Cummings had some, though they were not on view. They were in a cardboard box under his stall, with quite a lot of antiquities obviously from the 'Dorchester' hoard. Day could not remember if Cummings had himself referred to it as the 'Dorchester' hoard, but that was what it was called in the trade, and as Cummings had distributed it, then he assumed that Cummings had given it that name. Miss Smith was unimpressed: anyone could have given it that name. Day had been telephoned by Garriock, whom he had not previously known. Garriock had read an article that Day had written about Bronze Age antiquities. The 'Dorchester' hoard had been mentioned, and Garriock had said: 'Would it surprise you to know that I found it?' Day went to Garriock's house in Salisbury and was shown the antiquities that he had and the photographs of the hoard. Later he was taken to Rossiter's house and bought 10 or 15 antiquities from him for £500 or £600. Like everything else that he saw he had them photographed and passed the photographs to Andy Lawson. There was an allegation that he paid Garriock for providing the contact with Rossiter, but Day denied it. Garriock had indicated that the site could be seen from his house, and this is why Day had thought that it was at Bemerton. Day subsequently visited Rossiter — a social visit. He had been with his family on holiday in the West Country and had heard that Rossiter's marriage had broken up. Mrs Day had felt sorry for him so they had called in to see him.

Day photographed all the antiquities from the hoard that passed through his hands, including some that he had had on approval but had not bought. He had traded as a registered antiquities dealer (part-time) under the name of Peter Stannard. When Day's own marriage broke up he sold all his antiquities to a dealer called Goodwin, who passed them on to Cummings.

That took us to lunch-time, and I went off with Jack Woods and Andy Cockburn to the pub at the corner: the canteen in the court had not been impressive. The next witness was Julia Schottlander. Younger than I had expected, petite, somewhat Bohemian, she came in carrying a coat. It had happened so long ago that she could remember very little. She had known Cummings as a dealer for some time, and at one of the Cumberland Hotel fairs he had approached her about some Bronze Age antiquities. He knew that she was a friend of Maurice Braham, and thought that Braham would be interested in them. The antiquities were taken to her rooms in London, where Braham viewed them: but Braham did not meet Cummings there. There were more than 12 antiquities but not a great number: it was so long ago that she couldn't remember. Cummings had given her the provenance, which she passed on to Braham, but she could not now remember it. Apart from the complete antiquities there were three boxes — plastic ice-cream

that he would direct the jury to dismiss the charges.

Afterwards Cummings came over to me and said that in future we must cooperate more closely to avoid misunderstandings. He said that he was very surprised that we had missed the best two razors (fortunately I had our photographs and was able to get him to identify them) which had been in the McAlpine auction but we had not seen them. He knew that we had sent three people to view the sale, and he knew that we had managed to get a bronze gouge withdrawn. He had bid for the razors but had not bought them. It seemed a most unlikely story and later enquiries failed to substantiate it (p. 104), but at the time I was in no mood for discussing it further with him.

The case resumed on the Tuesday morning at 10.30, when the judge explained to the jury that as a result of legal arguments Cummings had no case to answer, so he directed them to dismiss the charges. Then, at 10.40, Garriock's counsel asked for 20 minutes to confer with his client. At 11 o'clock both Garriock and Rossiter pleaded guilty to the theft of the hoard from Mr Cook. The judge deferred sentences until 9 June by which time he would have received reports from the probation service. That was that. After the leisurely pace of proceedings over the last week the sudden end came as quite a shock. The unfortunate jury had had nothing to do.

I did not go to court on Friday, 9 June, I was away on holiday. But on the Monday morning Jack Woods phoned to tell me that Garriock and Rossiter had each been sentenced to nine months imprisonment suspended for a year.

The sentences provoked another round of publicity. A piece in *The Daily Telegraph* concluded:

> Judge Christopher Hordern told the two guilty men that they had been 'deliberately dishonest'. Their sentence, he said, should serve as a warning to other treasure hunters.

The Guardian quoted the judge at greater length:

> 'You had enough knowledge to appreciate that you had come across something that was of very considerable archaeological importance, and that if you did not report it to somebody the archaeological value of what you had found might well be considerably impaired, if not lost.' There was no doubt prison sentences had to be passed, but in view of the 'quite exceptional circumstances' they could

be suspended. Not only had a long time elapsed since they discovered what had since become known as the Salisbury Hoard, but he could understand 'the excitement and the degree of temptation which was placed before you'.

7. The Acquisition

The trial ended with the two metal detectorists being convicted of theft, but that was not the only result. It also showed the vulnerability of the dealers: a single lie at the very beginning of the chain led to even big West End dealers handling stolen property. And it provided a well-documented example of the complex movements of antiquities between dealers, auction houses, collectors and museums. But immediately its most significant result for the British Musuem was to establish that the Salisbury Hoard had been the property of Reginald Cook, so following his death it belonged to his estate.

The hoard had been scattered far and wide, but more than half of its known quantity, some 350 artefacts, had been seized by the police and was sitting in a strong-room in the British Museum. Now we had to build on the court's decision and see if we could keep it in the Museum. Our long-term aim was to acquire as many of the artefacts as possible, so that they could be stored together, made available to scholars, and exhibited to the general public. Indeed, we had reserved a case for them in our new Iron Age gallery, which was due to be opened more than two years after the end of the trial, in July 1997. But first we had to secure title.

The police wrote to all those from whom they had seized artefacts, explained that anyone wishing to make a claim must notify DCI Woods, and that if no claims were made the property would be returned to the Cook estate. McAlpine maintained his claim to the ownership of the remaining pieces of the 'Gloucestershire' hoard, but he returned it to the Cook estate as a gift. John Fowler pressed his claim, and reiterated that he was keen to keep a sample, but not the unique pieces, and he was willing to bequeath to the British Museum anything he was allowed to retain. In due course an agreement along these lines was formalised. Paul Robinson brought in the artefacts that he had kept on display at Devizes, and said that he had written to Mrs Lowrie in an attempt to retain them permanently. My own view was that everything should be curated in the British Museum: having everything together would facilitate study, and from that point of view the many fragments that Devizes had were most important because we might establish joins not only with existing pieces (indeed two had already been joined) but with those that might turn up in the future. Paul had played an important role, for without his actions many significant artefacts would have been scattered and lost. I sympathised with his position, and appreciated the local interest in the case, but perhaps that could be satisfied with the loan of pieces for exhibition, which was a regular practice.

The British Museum had purchased the miniature shields with the aid of a substantial grant from the National Heritage Memorial Fund. And we had agreed to refund the grant if McAlpine's title was found to be faulty. For some time George Morris had been worried that the deal might become subject to limitation, and he had written to McAlpine towards the end of 1994 to seek an assurance that our purchase price would be returned if it was found that the shields had been stolen. No such assurance was forthcoming, so the advice of the Treasury Solicitor was sought and we eventually consulted a barrister.

The problem was quite complex, depending on the interpretation of the 1980 Limitation Act, and in particular on one section that Counsel considered a particularly impenetrable piece of drafting. Stolen property that had changed hands several times becomes the property of the purchaser six years after the first innocent transaction. We decided to await the outcome of the trial, which eventually established that the first innocent transaction had been Cummings' purchase from Garriock and Rossiter in 1985. So it would seem that the Museum might have a claim to ownership, but the Trustees considered that it would be quite wrong to pursue it. Mrs Lowrie was told that we would not be making a claim but that we would retain custody of the miniature shields pending her instructions. The grant was re-paid to the National Heritage Memorial Fund. So one result of my researches was that the Museum lost £55,000.

The day after the trial *The Daily Telegraph* carried a report by Maurice Weaver, who had spent quite some time researching the case. He had interviewed McAlpine, who had said that he might be prepared to reimburse the Trustees of the British Museum if their legal ownership of the shields was successfully challenged. 'If it is found that the British Museum is going to lose out, I suppose my reaction would be to give my part back to them' (i.e. his half share of the miniature shields). But in the event his solicitors took a firm line and maintained that the expiry of the period of limitation gave the Museum legal title.

The Trustees asked Ian Longworth and me to make contact with the Lowries, and with Mr Oglethorpe, the executor of Mr Cook's estate. We went to see them in May and gave them photographs of the artefacts and a copy of our detailed inventory. The artefacts themselves were still at the British Museum. We spent a couple of hours chatting, answering questions on the archaeology, and discussing the future of the finds. From the first contact I had never made any secret of the Museum's aim to acquire the entire hoard, or at any rate as many pieces as could now be retrieved. The situation was complicated, inevitably. The hoard did not belong to the Lowries; it was part of the Cook estate which had not yet been settled because details of building and agricultural relief had to be sorted out before the amount of Inheritance Tax could be assessed. They were dealing not only with the old man's estate, but also with that of his wife, who had predeceased him by a year. The Cooks had held the land jointly, so Mrs Cook would have had a half share in the hoard, but at the time of her death no one knew that the hoard had been stolen from them: Oglethorpe wondered if this would affect her claim. He did not yet know how much tax was due on the two estates, but on the face of it he was keen to pursue the possibilities of handing over the hoard in lieu of Inheritance Tax. He had done this once before, for another client, and it would be tax efficient for the Lowries and beneficial to the British Museum and the nation. Moves on this front would take time, but the first stage would be for the executors to get an independent valuation of the hoard. He was reluctant to approach Sotheby's or Christie's, so I suggested Seaby's. Peter Clayton was as reliable as anyone when it came to valuing antiquities, and he was already familiar with the Salisbury Hoard.

The other matter that we raised was the proposed excavation after harvest. When we had finished the dig in November 1993 we had planned to return in 1994 to look at a more extensive area of the site. Then we decided to await the outcome of the trial, so I transferred the plans to 1995. But over the months circumstances had changed. In particular I was due to retire in January 1996 and other commitments were crowding in. One more season there was likely to raise more problems than it solved; this site needed a major campaign which was perhaps more appropriate to the local archaeological unit than the British Museum. I had to take a decision, and I decided not to excavate at Netherhampton. But I did leave the door open to the possibility of some more survey work in September.

One evening about a week after sentences had been passed, we got a telephone call at home. Sheelagh took it and thought that she recognised the voice, but not the name. It was Jim. Jim Garriock. She knew him as 'John'. He told me that he had no hard feelings and thought the outcome had been fair. I agreed. He'd heard that I was writing a book about the case, and suggested that he should be co-author. But I didn't see much scope for cooperation.

At the end of June Jack Woods came in to compare notes and clarify details while we could still remember them. As a result I drew up a list of outstanding queries and sent out another batch of letters. To Cavill to confirm the artefacts he had received as commission, and to find out whether he had sold them to Braham or Cummings: he replied promptly and said he had sold to Brian Grover, a new name for me. I wrote again to Andrew Sherratt: there was a persistent rumour that the Ashmolean had acquired Salisbury Hoard artefacts. He too responded promptly: they had nothing, so perhaps the rumours referred to their temporary exhibition of McAlpine's antiquities in 1987. I wrote to Christie's, because I had promised to keep them informed with regard to the antiquities held by Barbara Goldstein in Salt Lake City, and I enquired about another Salisbury Hoard piece (lot 10, sold 4 November 1992) that we had not traced. They responded that it had been purchased by a Frenchman, and they would make enquiries via their office in Paris, but I heard no more. And I wrote to Robin Symes, telling him that the batch of antiquities that the police had seized from him included seven flat axes from another source: we wanted to return them to him. I also asked for any information he had about the movement of the hoard, and in particular about two fine razors (the ones that Cummings had mentioned after the trial) that had been recorded at Norwich Castle Museum along with artefacts that had ended up in Symes' collection. I got nowhere with the queries, but eventually one of his staff called to collect the extraneous axes.

The disappearance of the two fine razors puzzled me. Cummings had been adamant that they had been included in the McAlpine sale, but Stuart hadn't seen them and there was no hint of them in the catalogue. I decided to take up Cummings' offer of closer cooperation, but he did not respond. However, shortly afterwards he did write to the Director, expressing his concern about my behaviour and actions in the course of my investigations into the Salisbury

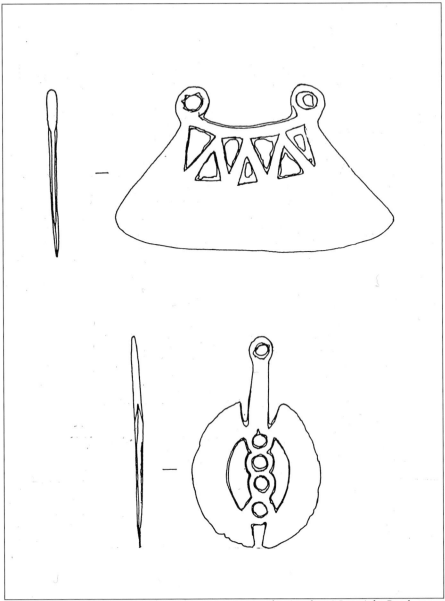

7   Record drawings of two bronze razors submitted to Norwich Castle Museum (full size). See also **Colour plate 16.**

Hoard. The matter that seemed to concern him most was the two missing razors. They had been handled by Peter Day and shown to Norwich Castle Museum, as recorded in my book. According to Cummings they were subsequently sold to Lord McAlpine, and included in the sale of his collection at Sotheby's. He noted, correctly, that three members of our Department's staff had viewed the sale, and that we had had a gouge from the Salisbury Hoard withdrawn. He insisted that we had failed to notice the two razors, and said that Sotheby's had confirmed in writing that at least one of them was definitely in the sale. Cummings suggested that we had deliberately overlooked the two items in order to protect Peter Day. That was nonsense. We looked again at the sale catalogue, but there was no hint of them, despite the fact that they were distinctive and more valuable than many other pieces individually described. Stuart took up the matter with Sotheby's, but got nowhere; they were unable to confirm or deny that the razors had been in the sale. An unsolved mystery.

One day those razors will surface, and I include here the Norwich drawings to aid identification **(Fig 7, and Colour plate 16)**. They are among at least 188 Salisbury Hoard artefacts now in private collections, and over the years several of them are bound to come to our notice. One day when Stuart was checking some old papers he came across records of two axes almost certainly from the Salisbury Hoard, but submitted to us before we had any documentation of it. The private collector who had brought them in had retained them still, and we were able to check them against the photographs and confirm the provenance.

In December 1995 Oglethorpe phoned to say that they were at last finalising the tax position of the Cook estate. Mrs Lowrie was proposing to offer the miniature shields in lieu of tax, and he wanted me to provide full details of them so that he could inform the tax authorities. But she had yet to decide the fate of the rest of the hoard.

I retired from the Museum the following month, handing over my Salisbury Hoard files to Stuart. But there was little that he could do other than wait. Oglethorpe's papers went through to the Treasury, who sought the advice of the Department of National Heritage and the Museums and Galleries Commission. Three independent academics were invited to assess the importance of the hoard and submit reports. Before the end of 1996 it was obvious that our permanent exhibition in the new Iron Age gallery would have to go ahead without provision for the Salisbury Hoard. Shortly after the exhibition opened, in July 1997, we heard on the grape-vine that the papers had started their return journey, from the Museums and Galleries Commission to the Department of National Heritage (now re-named the Department of Culture, Media and Sport) where the Minister approved them in December. Papers were exchanged with the Cook estate, the deal was finalised, and in March 1998 the Minister decided that the antiquities should go to the British Museum.

It had taken a long time: 13 years after Garriock and Rossiter had discovered them, and 10 years after Lord McAlpine showed them to me, the British Museum finally acquired the 22 miniature shields. As part of the same deal, in lieu of Inheritance Tax, they also acquired 19 antiquities accumulated by John Fowler; he is to retain 8 others during his lifetime but will bequeath them to a museum. So we are home and dry with 41 antiquities from the Salisbury Hoard, but what about the other 500 or so? More than 300 antiquities are in the possession of Mrs Lowrie, and she has yet to decide on their future. In England antiquities (other than gold, silver and associated artefacts) are the property of whoever owns the land at the time of their discovery. The landowner is entitled to do what he likes with them: he can display them on the mantlepiece, for instance, or give them away as Christmas presents, or throw them in the dustbin, or allow a museum to acquire them. Fortunately most landowners settle for this last option. That leaves at least 188 artefacts, a third of the hoard, still in the possession of persons unknown. I hope that the publication of this book will bring some of them to light, and that any information about them will be passed to Stuart Needham, at the British Museum.

Postscript

In June 1998, as this book goes to press, Mrs Lowrie has offered to sell her artefacts from the Salisbury Hoard to the British Museum.

SALISBURY HOARD: provisional numbers of artefacts			
Axes	flat	4	
	flanged	6	
	palstaves	9	
	socketed	173	192
Missile points	spearheads	46	
	arrowheads	1	47
Daggers, etc	rapiers	4	
	dirks	3	
	socketed dagger	1	
	unclassified	1	9
Chapes		7	7
Knives	tanged	12	
	socketed	8	
	notched butt	7	
	miscellaneous	10	37
Tools	chisels, tanged	29	
	lugged	2	
	socketed	3	
	flanged	2	
	gouges, socketed	30	
	socketed tools	4	
	hammers, socketed	5	
	looped ?	1	
	punches, awls, etc.	11	
	anvil	1	
	sickles	2	90
Toilet	razors	17	
	tweezers	1	18
Dress	pins	16	16
Miniatures	shields	24	
	cauldrons	46	
	socketed axe	1	
	? currency bar	1	72
Miscellaneous	cones 4; ferrules 9: 'moustaches' 2; pendant 1; buttons 5; discs 7.	28	
	ornamental fragments	10	
	others	17	
	waste	6	
	hone-stone	1	62
	TOTAL		535

8   Classification of artefacts from the Salisbury Hoard: provisional numbers.

gives a total of 535 artefacts. More than a third of them, 160, were axes and the vast majority of those were socketed axes.

The evolution of the Bronze Age axe provides one of the classic typologies of European prehistory, and the main stages are represented in the Salisbury Hoard **(Colour plate 17)**. Earliest are the four flat axes, that would have been cast by pouring molten bronze into an open mould made by hollowing the shape of the axe in a flat surface, often a stone. One of the four is likely to have been made of copper, before it was appreciated that a more durable tool or weapon could be made of bronze by alloying the copper with about 10% tin. One of the earliest metal axes from Britain, it is certainly the earliest artefact from the Salisbury Hoard and dates from about 2400 BC. The next stage in the axe typology, also represented here by four examples, is the flanged axe, whose sides were raised to help to secure the haft. Flanged axes were in use from about 1700 BC for 600 years or so and were gradually replaced by the more elaborate palstaves. The palstave — there were nine in the Salisbury Hoard — has the flanges linked by a prominent ridge across the middle to provide a stop for the haft, and ultimately a loop at the side to help to secure the thong that would have lashed the axe-head to its haft. Flanged axes and palstaves would have required more complex bivalve moulds whose two halves themselves were sometimes cast in bronze. The final 'stage' in the development, the socketed axe, was introduced as early as 1400 BC and became the dominant axe type from about 1100 BC. It remained in use until the eighth century BC, by which time iron had replaced bronze as the principal metal for tools and weapons.

The majority of the 173 socketed axes in the Salisbury Hoard were not, however, functional tools. When new the 141 'tinned' axes would have shone brightly, like silver. They have sockets that are oval in plan and fairly straight sides that expand slightly to the blade. Most of them are decorated on both faces with arrangements of vertical ribs and dots. But they are unfinished: they still have a rough edge down both sides of the socket, where the molten metal penetrated between the two halves of the mould. On a normal axe this rough edge would be removed in the finishing process, when the casting was cleaned and the blade sharpened. But the failure to finish the 'tinned' axes was not a matter of chance, it was part of the original design. The alloy was such that the axes could never have been used: they were so brittle that they would have shattered at the first blow. Such unfinished 'tinned' axes are not unique to the Salisbury Hoard, and associations show that they belong to the very end of the sequence of Bronze Age axes.

They are contemporary with the Armorican socketed axe, which has straight sides without any expansion at the blade, is always unfinished, has an alloy with more lead and less tin than the Salisbury Hoard axes, and is found by the thousand in hoards in Brittany and Normandy. One Armorican hoard is thought to have had about 4000 of these axes, and several had more than 500. The axes in the Armorican hoards were usually stacked neatly, recalling the description of the Salisbury Hoard, though of course the most efficient way of burying a large number of artefacts in a small hole would be to pack them carefully. Some had the axes in a circular arrangement with the sockets on the outside and the blades on edge, meeting in the centre. Armorican axes were distributed elsewhere in north-west Europe, reaching England and even Ireland: a hoard of six was found at Nether Wallop, Hampshire, 22km (13½ miles) from Netherhampton. If it was impossible to use them, if it had never been intended that they should be functional axes, what purpose did they serve? Some have suggested that they were ingots, a convenient way of trading and storing metal, but others reject any economic function and regard them as dedications to a god.

Other Bronze Age artefacts include 46 spearheads; 9 daggers, rapiers or dirks; 7 chapes; 37 knives; 90 tools - especially chisels and gouges; 17 razors; and 16 pins **(Fig 8)**.

The most distinctive Iron Age artefacts in the hoard are the miniature shields **(Figs 1 and 2, and Colour plate 1)**. Before the discovery of the Salisbury Hoard only 15 miniature shields were known from Iron Age Britain, and all of them were oval or rectangular in shape. Of the 24 found in the Salisbury Hoard, only two were oval and the rest were 'hide-shaped', with convex sides and concave ends, a form of shield hitherto unknown. But once the miniatures had been seen it was possible to identify fragments of the bronze bindings of full-sized shields of the same type. These shields would have been made of wood and leather, which would have perished long ago, but they had bindings of bronze whose distinctive corners are known from 13 sites in southern England.

It is typical of the chance element in archaeology that only six months after the miniature shields surfaced the remains of a complete hide-shaped shield were found in a grave at Deal in Kent. The Deal grave dates from about 200 BC, and other fragments of these shields belong to the first century BC. Judging from the bindings, hide-shaped shields were relatively common in Iron Age Britain, and it seems that they were quite effective, too. One of the groups interested in battle re-enactment and 'living history', the Vectis Iron Age Society, has experimented with the form and enthuses about it. It is relatively light, gives improved visibility, can be used also as a weapon and to pin opponents to the ground, and can even serve as a seat (like a shooting stick).

The models are from 44mm (1¾in) to 103mm (4in) high, which compares with 1.19m (almost 4ft) for the full length of the Deal shield. They are accurate copies of the functional shield, to the extent that all have tiny handles riveted to the back and one has a separate binding. The life-sized versions are likely to have been made of wood or leather, with the binding and perhaps the handle being the only metal components and the only pieces that in normal circumstances would survive burial in the ground. Five of the Salisbury miniatures had been decorated, which implies that some of the full-sized shields were also decorated. On the miniatures the decoration is engraved or chased in metal, but the working shields were doubtless painted on wood and any trace of the paint, indeed any trace of the wood, has long since disappeared.

There are at least 46 miniature cauldrons in the Salisbury Hoard, small vessels made of sheet bronze and provided with two ring-handles **(Fig 9)**. On average they are 42mm (just over 1½in) in diameter and 13mm (½in) deep, but they range from 18mm (¾in) to 70mm (2¾in) with depths from a half to a fifth of the diameter. The deeper examples are obviously modelled on cauldrons and some have upright or slightly inturned rims defined by grooves, but others have more open, flared, rims and the shallower pieces seem more remote from cauldrons. However, some of the shallower pieces are very well made, and there is no obvious break between the two extremes of the range. The handles are simple rings, usually butted pieces of wire, attached by small riveted mounts, split-pin mounts (some with ring-handles cut from sheet bronze) or simply threaded directly through perforations in the sides of the vessels. Four of the cauldrons have handle mounts in the form of perforated projections rising above the rim. The outsides of the vessels have been polished, but several have tool-marks on the inside, where they have been raised from the sheet bronze. Most rims have been simply cut, but some have been folded over to strengthen them. Two cauldrons have been repaired in antiquity, with riveted patches like those on one of the miniature shields.

It seems likely that the bronze vessels are miniatures of full-size functional pieces, but their precise prototype is not as obvious as the shields'. They are simple rounded vessels with few distinctive

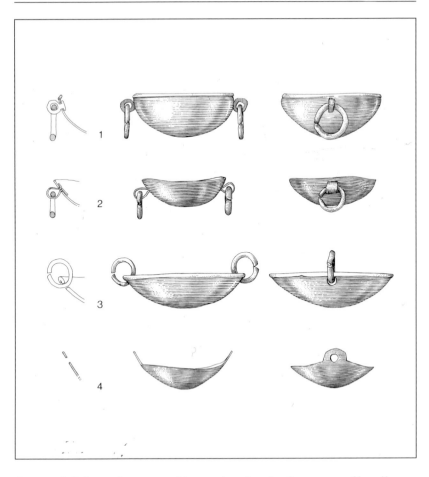

9   Miniature bronze cauldrons, showing the four types of handle
       (full size). Drawn by Karen Hughes.

features other than the pair of handles. Bronze vessels first appear
north of the Alps in the later Bronze Age, and several cauldrons of
that date are known from the British Isles. But they are distinctive
vessels with everted rims and bodies made of several sheets joined by
lines of large dome-headed rivets, and they do not resemble the
Salisbury Hoard miniatures. The latest of these vessels are found in
hoards dating from the very beginning of the Iron Age in the seventh
century BC. No complete British cauldron can be dated accurately in
the following centuries, not until the first century BC. Even on the
continent there are few complete cauldrons from the sixth to the
second century, but those few are simpler than the Late Bronze Age
types. In particular the two cauldrons from the second-century

116

deposit at La Tène, in Switzerland, bear some resemblance to the Salisbury Hoard vessels: one has an open profile with sloping sides, and the other is almost hemispherical with slightly inturned rim. Cauldrons in the first century BC are similar but more globular, and subsequent Roman cauldrons often have quite vertical necks. Although the evidence is slight, it is not inconsistent with dating the miniature cauldrons to about the same time as the miniature shields.

Miniature cauldrons are extremely rare. There are two simple pieces in the 'Batheaston' hoard (p. 120), each with a pair of perforations but no surviving handle; perhaps they are cauldrons, though they would never have been accepted as such but for some of the examples in the Salisbury Hoard. Otherwise there are only two undoubted miniature cauldrons from Britain, one from Lincolnshire and the other from Grampian, both modelled on Roman cauldrons.

There may be other Iron Age miniatures in the Salisbury Hoard. A very small and crude socketed axe is the best contender, and there is a suggestion that miniatures of Late Bronze Age axes were used in the Iron Age. Another piece might be a miniature currency bar, though if so it is without parallel. And the ferrules acquired from Peter Day bear a resemblance to miniatures, though quite what they represent is a mystery. As for other Iron Age objects in the Salisbury Hoard, there are no distinctive types, but several oddities might belong here rather than in the Bronze Age. In particular, there is the curious 'moustache' object that appeared in McAlpine's 'Gloucestershire' hoard, and what seems like half of a similar object. Their date and purpose remain unknown, but two precisely similar pieces have been found by metal detectorists in recent years.

The miniature shields and cauldrons are small-scale models of the shields and cauldrons used by Iron Age Britons. They may be compared with other metal models of weapons, tools and other objects found in Iron Age and Roman contexts in Britain and in Europe. Such models could have been toys, but many of them have been found at temple sites and it seems likely that they were votive. In Greek Orthodox churches small metal models are still used today: frequently they represent parts of the human body such as a leg, arm, eye or ear, and they indicate that the worshipper either requires help to cure the ailing part, or gives thanks for a successful cure. Some of the models found at ancient temples might be viewed in this light, or they might be more specific attributes of a particular god.

Shields and cauldrons could be taken to reflect two major concerns of primitive peoples, concerns that might warrant the intercession of the gods. The shield could be seen as an attribute of warfare, or perhaps protection from warfare, whilst the cauldron could represent food. There are hints that bronze cauldrons were highly prized in European Iron Age communities, as when the Cimbri tribe sent 'the most sacred cauldron in their country' as a diplomatic gift to the Emperor Augustus. And in early Irish literature, regarded as 'a window on the Iron Age' though committed to writing several centuries later, bronze cauldrons held a prominent place and sometimes had magical properties.

The Salisbury Hoard is important because of its very size. Almost 600 bronze artefacts buried together in a pit. It was deposited in the Iron Age, and it included more artefacts than any other Iron Age hoard found in Britain. But most of those artefacts were made in the Bronze Age, and numerically they are surpassed by only one other British Bronze Age hoard — a hoard actually deposited in the Bronze Age — found at Isleham, Cambridgeshire, in 1959. Before the days of metal detectorists, the Isleham Hoard was unearthed in the way that antiquities have been disovered for centuries, by a farmer ploughing his field. Archaeologists were alerted, and the following year, after harvest, an excavation was organised and the rest of the deposit was recovered. The hoard had been buried in a pot, which had been deposited in a pit about 12in (30cm) across at the bottom and cut 14in (35cm) into the chalk. Within the pot there had been about 6500 pieces of bronze weighing some 200lb (90kg): about 10 times the number of pieces and perhaps twice the weight of the Salisbury Hoard. But a simple numerical comparison is misleading, because much of the Isleham hoard was scrap bronze. Of the 6500 pieces, 2600 were broken fragments of raw metal plate, and the rest were complete or fragmentary weapons, tools and ornaments, some deliberately broken before depositon. The excavators interpreted this find as scrap assembled by a metal-worker and buried for safe-keeping until he was ready to put it in the melting pot for re-cycling. It had been buried about 1000 BC.

In terms of size the Salisbury Hoard is very impressive, but more important is the chronology of its artefacts. The earliest piece was made about 2400 BC and the latest piece no earlier than 200 BC. Between those two dates there is scarcely a century that is not represented by a Salisbury Hoard artefact. An extensive hoard with a date range of 2200 years is quite without parallel. Isleham is much more typical, covering no more than a hundred years. Indeed the chronology of prehistory is based on the assumption that associated artefacts are more or less contemporary in date, and only rarely does a metalwork hoard include an occasional much earlier piece.

But there are hints of the same phenomenon elsewhere in Iron Age Britain, including a group of bronzes excavated recently at the hillfort at Danebury in Hampshire. The term 'hoard' needs some qualification here, because the artefacts were scattered. The first piece was found in 1974 in the roots of a tree that had blown down; 11 more were in an area subsequently excavated, but they were in soil that had been disturbed by tree roots and burrowing animals; seven others found nearby seemed to have been eroded from the original deposit in antiquity; and one was subsequently found in re-deposited top-soil. The excavator argued convincingly that these 20 artefacts had originally been deposited as a single hoard. There were 7 axes, 2 spearheads (one a fragment), 2 rapiers (one a fragment), part of a sword and part of a knife, 4 chisels, 2 razors and a pin. The dates of the artefacts ranged between 1800 and 600 BC, with two in the first half and six in the second half of the second millennium and the rest in the first millennium BC.

There may have been a similar deposit at Hounslow, London, but the accounts of the discovery are obscure. In 1864 labourers working in a field discovered a collection of Bronze Age and Iron Age antiquities. They were taken to the British Museum where the Keeper of the Department of British and Medieval Antiquities, A. W. Franks, was told that all the antiquities had been found together. But on further enquiry it transpired that two groups of artefacts (one Bronze Age and the other Iron Age) had come from different parts of the same field. The Museum acquired the artefacts in two lots, with Bronze Age and Iron Age pieces in each lot, and in the 1930s a subsequent curator, Christopher Hawkes, annotated the Register to distinguish two hoards, one Bronze Age and the other Iron Age, on typological grounds. The Iron Age element, comprising five animal figurines, a wheel ornament and the remains of a crown, is usually regarded as a religious deposit **(Colour plate 18)**. One wonders if the archaeologists simplified and rationalised the evidence, persuading the labourers that the Iron Age and Bronze Age artefacts could never have been found together. If so, the rationalisation is not too successful, because the Bronze Age element alone has an amazing chronological range, including Early, Middle and Late Bronze Age pieces spanning more than a thousand years. Viewed in the context of the Salisbury Hoard, Hounslow seems very similar indeed, and like Salisbury the sequence ends with religious artefacts in the Iron Age.

At Hagbourn Hill, in Berkshire, a similar mixed group of artefacts was found in 1803. The account of the discovery is not as clear as we would now like, but there is no doubt that Bronze Age and Iron Age artefacts had been buried together. Of the surviving pieces there are three spearheads, two pins and a palstave from the Bronze Age, and a socketed axe was illustrated in the original account. Iron Age pieces still preserved comprise parts of two horse-bits, three terrets (rein-rings) and a ring-headed pin. There are said to have been some coins, as well, including a large flat gold coin that might be correlated with a surviving gold stater recorded as found in that parish in 1803.

But the closest parallel for the Salisbury Hoard in terms of its size and chronological range is the 'Batheaston' hoard, a remarkable collection of antiquities purchased at a Sotheby's sale by the British Museum. Lot 220 in the antiquities sale on 22 May 1989 was 'a collection of Bronze Age artifacts, mostly circa 2000-1800 BC, including Stop-Ridge and Socketed Celts, Spearheads, Dagger Blades, Chisels and Other Items. (a lot)', and the estimate was £3000 to £4000. One of my colleagues saw them, or some of them, and was particularly interested in a rare group of Early Bronze Age bronzes. The Museum bid successfully and was pleased to get them for a hammer price of £2000. But it was only when we went to collect them that we realised the extent of our purchase: there was indeed a lot, a lot more than we had seen.

At first sight it seemed to be a miscellaneous collection of metal detectorist finds, but as we looked closer we could see that it had been sorted. There was nothing medieval, and nothing Roman. There were Early Bronze Age and Middle Bronze Age pieces from the second millennium BC, but many more from the first millennium, ranging from 800 or 900 BC down to about 300 BC. One very surprising feature was the large number of Late Bronze Age and Iron Age pins: more than had hitherto been recorded from the entire country. Yet the collection was surely British. Indeed, some of the brooches were of a type current only in the Wessex area. These artefacts could never have been assembled by an antiquities collector: the lower chronological limit was too precise (even if a collector had been interested only in Bronze Age and Iron Age antiquities he would surely have included some later Iron Age pieces) and pins are very rarely available on the market. It was not a site collection: no prehistoric site would produce such a range and richness of bronze artefacts. Could it be a hoard, or several hoards? That seemed the most likely explanation, though pins and brooches very rarely occur in hoards.

Sotheby's declined to reveal the name of the vendor, though they did say that they believed that the antiquities had been found near

'BATHEASTON' HOARD				
Axes	palstaves		5	
	socketed		2	7
Missile points	spearheads:	tanged	1	
		socketed	1	
	arrowhead		1	3
Daggers			2	2
Chape			1	1
Knives			4	4
Tools	chisels, tanged		8	
	gouges, socketed		2	
	awls, etc.		16	26
Toilet	tweezers		3	3
Dress	Pins:	straight shanks	94	
		swans-neck	44	138
	Brooches:	La Tène I	11	
		pennanular	30	
		others	3*	44
Miniatures	cauldrons ?		2	2
Looped buttons			6	
Small rings			35	41
Miscellaneous	triskeles 2; wheel pendant 1; pendant disc 1; binding 1; discs attached to wires 2; riveted boss 1; looped disc 1; studs 2; unclassified 19		30	30
			TOTAL	301
	* one brooch lost			

10   Classification of artefacts from the 'Batheaston' Hoard.

Batheaston, Bath. They offered to forward a letter to the vendor, but that brought no response. Three years later, in 1992, we identified a second batch of antiquities from the same 'hoard', in the possession of a London collector, and a year after that a metal detectorist gave me more information including photographs of some of the pieces. Two dealers were also able to help. But the story of the discovery is still incomplete. Found by two metal detectorists, the antiquities had been in a pit about 18in (45cm) deep: there was a confusing references to a second pit, so perhaps two separate hoards were found. It seems that the site was in south Wiltshire, probably in the vicinity of Wylye, about 15km (9½ miles) from where the Salisbury Hoard was found. And it is likely that the hoard(s) was removed without the landowners' knowledge, perhaps from a scheduled ancient monument.

The chronological range of the 'Batheaston' hoard is impressive, but it is about 1000 years shorter than the Salisbury Hoard. Its earliest artefacts were made about 1600 BC and the latest, La Tène I brooches, about 300 BC. The total, 301, is about half the number of artefacts found in the Salisbury Hoard. And there are significant differences in the concentrations of artefact types. The 'Batheaston' hoard has far fewer axes, spearheads, and blades; and fewer chisels and gouges, although there are rather more awls and similar small tools. Instead the 'Batheaston' hoard is dominated by personal ornaments: almost 10 times as many pins, and 44 brooches — a type not recorded in the Salisbury Hoard **(Fig 10, cf Fig 8)**. The counterpart to the votive miniatures that terminate the Salisbury hoard is a minor element at 'Batheaston': two possible miniature cauldrons and a wheel pendant. The two miniature cauldrons are hemispherical in shape, made of sheet bronze, and they have a couple of perforations near the edge on opposing sides. But for the Salisbury Hoard they would have been classified as unidentified bronzes, but similar pieces at Salisbury are undoubtedly cauldrons. Another link between the two hoards is provided by a socketed spearhead whose tip has been worn down to such an extent that the hollow interior has been exposed. Stuart Needham tells me that he knows of only two similar pieces: one was found in the Salisbury Hoard, and the other in the second hoard (Hoard B) that we excavated at Netherhampton.

Individually all the examples quoted are unsatisfactory. Only the Danebury 'hoard' was excavated by archaeologists, and it had been scattered before they found it; the accounts of Hounslow, Hagbourn Hill and 'Batheaston' are in parts obscure. But collectively they are more impressive, and they suggest that the Salisbury Hoard was not the only collection of Bronze Age and Iron Age artefacts that spanned several centuries. How can it be explained?

Today any individual's possessions are likely to date within 50 or 60 years of one another, unless he is a collector of antiques or antiquities. Could it be that the Salisbury Hoard was the collection of an antiquities dealer? One of Lord McAlpine's 'runners', who for some reason decided to bury his collection? Feasible, but far-fetched. The sequence of antiquities lasts for over two thousand years and comes to a sudden end in the second century BC, so it is more reasonable to suppose that they were buried about that time rather than later.

Perhaps it was assembled by a prehistoric collector of antiquities — the original Alpine, the Ancient Briton?

The latest artefacts in the hoard help to assess its date: certainly it was not buried before 200 BC, and probably not much later. They also provide a clue to the reason for its assemblage. The latest artefacts are the miniature shields, perhaps also the miniature cauldrons, and their function was religious. It may be that whoever collected the bronzes was motivated by religious beliefs. Perhaps Netherhampton was the centre of a religious cult that existed for a couple of millennia, and the hoard is of holy relics. The miniatures (circa 200 BC) had a religious function, and perhaps the 'tinned' socketed axes (circa 700 BC), too, but other pieces are ordinary utilitarian weapons, tools, and ornaments. There is no reason to suppose that any of the Salisbury Hoard artefacts that date from the second millennium BC were manufactured purely for religious reasons.

An alternative, and much more likely, explanation is that members of the Iron Age community, around 200 BC, in the course of their daily work, chanced to find several hoards of Bronze Age artefacts. How many hoards is unknown, though when we come to study the antiquities in detail it may be possible to hazard a guess. The Iron Age farmers were continually disturbing the earth: ploughing the fields, erecting boundaries, digging drainage ditches and storage pits. A modern farmer would be most unlikely to discover several Bronze Age hoards, but in Iron Age times all operations were carried out by hand, so the workers were closer to the earth and had more time to observe; there's no knowing the extent of the territory over which the hoards were discovered, nor the number of years involved in their discovery; and, of course, there must have been more Bronze Age hoards awaiting discovery in 200 BC than in AD 1985. If an Iron Age farmer found a hoard of Bronze Age bronzes, why did he not melt it down and re-cycle it? Perhaps most of them did. But perhaps someone who discovered a Bronze Age hoard in the vicinity of Salisbury was puzzled by it. He would have realised that he was handling axes, spearheads and knives that were quite different from those used in his own community. Conceivably he might have related them to his ancestors, or perhaps more likely he or the elders of his tribe would have regarded them as a signal from the gods. Such a hoard could have been treasured, and subsequent similar discoveries kept with it. There is an intriguing reference in Suetonius' *Life of Galba*: 'lightening struck a lake of Cantabria and twelve axes were found there, an unmistakable token of supreme power'. Perhaps that is an account of the discovery of an ancient hoard. The Bronze Age hoards found by Iron Age farmers near Salisbury could have been kept for superstitious or religious reasons, and eventually buried for reasons unknown.

PART II THE DISCOVERY AND PROTECTION OF ANTIQUITIES

9. Provenance

The story of the Salisbury Hoard shows how easily that collection of antiquities could have lost the provenance and context that made it so significant. It is important because it is a spectacular example, extremely well documented, but it is not an isolated case.

Antiquities, artefacts created by ancient men and women, are the life-blood of prehistory. The study of antiquities is the only way in which prehistorians can learn about people in the days before the written word. The same approach is essential in early historical times, as history slowly replaced prehistory, and even in more recent historical times the study of antiquities will supplement and balance the written record. Antiquities may be admired for their beauty and for the craftsmanship of their creators, but they are of very limited value unless we know where they were found (provenance) and, ideally, what was found with them (context).

A dramatic example of the importance of provenance and context is provided by some sherds of red-glazed Arretine pottery excavated by Sir Mortimer Wheeler in 1945. Arretine ware was manufactured in central Italy early in the first century AD, and distributed throughout the Roman Empire. Had he been digging in Italy, France, or even in southern England its discovery would have occasioned little surprise. But Wheeler was digging in southern India. The *provenance* of the Arretine ware showed that he was excavating a trading post which had had direct or indirect links with Italy about the time of Jesus Christ; and as it had been found in layers stratified with local finds, its *context* provided for the first time a fixed chronological point in the development of prehistoric south Indian pottery.

But while archaeologists use artefacts to write prehistory, other people collect artefacts as philatelists collect postage stamps. They want to own them and admire them, but they pay little regard to where they came from. Thus Wheeler's Arretine pot, had it been a complete example, would have been snapped up by a collector and placed in a show-case, and it would have mattered not a jot whether it was found in southern India, southern England, or Arezzo itself.

This approach to antiquities is followed by the auction houses and dealers as well as collectors. The antiquities dealer operates in the same way as his colleagues who trade in antiques and pictures. He sees a fine piece in an auction, or in the rooms of another dealer, and he buys it because he likes it, or because he knows a collector who would like it. The place where it was found is of very little significance and the majority of antiquities in auctions and in dealers cabinets are unprovenanced. So archaeologists have problems with the trade; or, to put it another way, the trade has problems with archaeologists. And those problems are compounded by the secrecy that surrounds the trade. The auction catalogue rarely gives the name of the vendor and the names of purchasers are never published. Auction houses and dealers protect the privacy of their clients, which obstructs the archaeologist who is keen to establish the provenance of an artefact. And it opens the door to a criminal element. It is not uncommon for antiquities to change hands many times, and it is impossible to make exhaustive enquiries about ownership at each stage. It is easy for stolen antiquities to enter the trade, and difficult for a dealer to establish that he has acquired good title. Indeed, it can be very difficult for a museum to establish that beyond doubt. Unlike stolen antiques and pictures, the first legal owner of an antiquity probably has no record of it. Antiquities in the earth belong to the landowner or the State, depending on the country in question: if they are stolen direct from the earth the owner has no knowledge of their existence. The archaeologist in his search for provenance may well discover stolen property.

The problem has been highlighted recently with major public exhibitions organised by respectable museums and galleries. Early in 1994 the Royal Academy mounted an exhibition of the George Oritz collection, a magnificent assemblage of antiquities of which about 90% were unprovenanced. Six months later the Getty Museum at Malibu showed the Lawrence Fleischman Collection. Of 295 catalogued entries, 85% were unprovenanced and only three were described as coming from a specific location. The loss to knowledge represented by just these two collections is enormous.

But the problem is more than academic. Why are there no provenances? Perhaps because some of the exhibits are fakes, but almost certainly because most of them have been illegally exported from their country of origin: they have been looted from archaeological sites, and stolen from their rightful owners. Throughout the world countries are becoming increasingly conscious of the importance of their antiquities, and laws are enacted to prevent their exportation. Strict laws prevent the legal exportation of antiquities, but unfortunately they also encourage the black market. Every year hundreds of valuable antiquities leave the Mediterranean countries, for instance, for the cabinets of rich collectors: and every one of them has lost the provenance and context that might have told us so much.

One outstanding recent example is the 'Sevso' treasure, 14 pieces of late Roman silver plate, purchased by Peter Wilson, former Chairman of Sotheby's, and the Earl of Northampton, early in the 1980s. It was an investment that they wanted to realise by selling at public auction, and a substantial investment, too, because the low estimate was $70 million. The provenance, even the country of origin, was unknown and Sotheby's contacted every country that had been in the Roman Empire, to see if the treasure was known as stolen property. And, of course, there was no record of it. The treasure was taken to the USA, and there it was seized and the sale was stopped. It was a national treasure, but of which nation? The Lebanon, Hungary, and Croatia all claimed it, but all lacked proof. The case continues, and the treasure resides in a bank vault. It is unlikely that the truth will ever be known, and the Sevso treasure will never hold its rightful place in history.

Most antiquities in our museums do have a provenance, but even in England unprovenanced antiquities have been around for a long time, and sadly their numbers are increasing. In the past an antiquity often lost its provenance for a quite innocent reason, such as carelessness or a failure to appreciate its importance. The man who found it knew where it came from, and he might well have passed that information to the museum, collector or dealer who bought it. In most museums that information would then have been safe, but collectors and dealers are another matter. As collectors sell and exchange their antiquities at each move there is a danger that the provenance will be lost. The conscientious collector might label the antiquity, but rarely does he mark it direct. At best he uses an adhesive label, which fades over the years and becomes detached. Separate labels are even more of a problem because they can be separated from the artefact they describe and associated with another one.

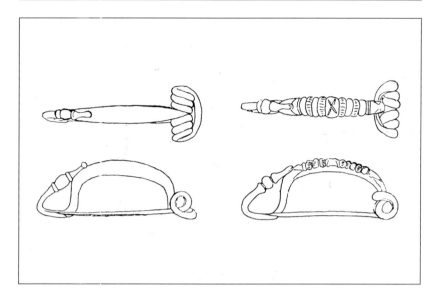

11   Bronze brooches, said to be from Wallingford (full size).
        Drawn by, or for, W. Page.

The ultimate result of the carelessness is a loss of information, and because we know so little about our antiquities any loss is to be deplored. Worse than the antiquity without a provenance is the one that has achieved a false provenance: this is not merely a loss of information, it is a step towards the distortion of history. If the database is limited the odd inaccurate fact can make a significant difference, and in the period that particularly concerns me — the British Iron Age — the database is very limited indeed.

Take, for example, a couple of bronze brooches from Wallingford in Berkshire, now in Reading Museum **(Fig 11)**. They were manufactured on the continent in the fourth century BC, and until recently they were virtually alone in providing evidence for direct contact between Britain and Europe at that time. Evidence for invaders, settlers or traders, perhaps. The brooches belong to a very distinctive type named after an important hoard from Duchcov (Dux) in Bohemia where no fewer than 2000 objects, mainly brooches and bracelets, were discovered in a cauldron on the site of a well. The Wallingford brooches are so precisely similar to the Duchov brooches that they might indeed have been part of that hoard. Perhaps they were. When first published, in 1906, no provenance was given but it was recorded that they had been in the collection of a Mr Davies, of Wallingford. Two years later another publication had them 'found at Wallingford ... nothing is known of the circumstances of their discovery' and by 1927 they were 'from the Thames at Wallingford'. Their status as provenanced continental imports was then unquestioned for over half a century. But there were warnings in the literature. The 1906 publication had suggested 'it is conceivable that some [of the brooches in the Davies Collection] were obtained from the Continent'. A later writer considered that Davies 'made his purchases without a too critical inquiry into their source' and another suspected that he was 'supplied with coins by persons who gave spurious provenances to pieces which they hoped to sell to him'. Davies might well have been gullible, but he himself never claimed that the two brooches had been found at Wallingford. That provenance was created by careless archaeologists. The Duchcov hoard was discovered in January 1882, and parts of it were rapidly dispersed by dealers and collectors. Some reached England, certainly by 1891 when 32 brooches were sold at Sotheby's in London. The two brooches from the Davies Collection, first recorded in November 1883 almost two years after the Duchov discovery, might well have come from Bohemia not in the fourth century BC but in the nineteenth century AD.

Potentially more dramatic than the Wallingford brooches is the bronze helmet from Charlbury in Oxfordshire, a type current in Italy about the time of the Celtic invasion **(Fig 12)**. Perhaps an Italian warrior had found his way to Britain early in the fourth century BC. According to a London dealer, Michel Dumez-Onof, who offered to sell the helmet to the British Museum, it had been found in Oxfordshire in 1892. Dumez-Onof had bought it from another dealer, Maurice Braham (who featured in the story of the Salisbury Hoard), who is said to have bought it from an unknown collector. At some stage the helmet is said to have belonged to the Hon Robert Erskine, archaeologist, television producer and collector. The trail led back to another dealer, Sandy Martin, who had first seen the helmet on the hall table at Cornbury Park, Charlbury, a country house then owned by the brewing magnate, Oliver Watney. It had been in a glass case (as it was when Dumez-Onof showed it to me) accompanied by a label recording a local provenance — but Martin could not recall the details and the label had since disappeared. Martin purchased the helmet a few years before Christie's sold some of the contents of Cornbury Park following the death of Oliver Watney in 1966.

As far as Martin could remember there were no other antiquities in the house, and he said that Oliver Watney had no interest whatsoever in antiquities. But Oliver's father, Vernon James Watney, who had purchased Cornbury Park in 1901, was more of an

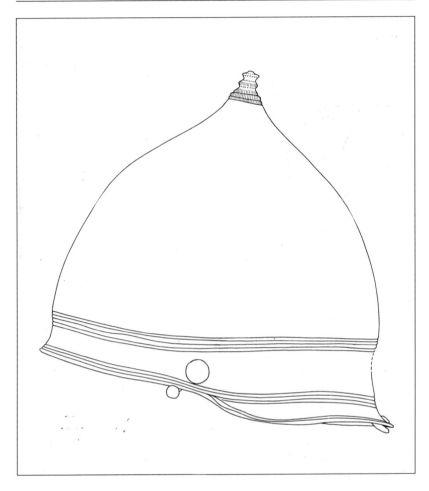

12   Bronze helmet from the Watney Collection (scale ½).
        Drawn by Robert Pengelly.

antiquary. Indeed, he had been elected a Fellow of the Society of Antiquaries of London in 1908, and two years later had written a large volume on the history of Cornbury and the Forest of Wychwood. His publication records local earthworks, and even a small coin of Constantine found near Charlbury in 1907, but there is no mention of the bronze helmet allegedly found in 1892. In the book there is a photograph of the drawing room at Cornbury Park, and in the background can be seen a glass case very like the one now housing the helmet. It is impossible to identify the object then in the case, but it is certainly not the helmet.

My colleague Mavis Bimson knew the Watney family and

mentioned our interest in the helmet to Mrs Gifford, Vernon Watney's grand-daughter. Mrs Gifford remembered it well, and referred to it as the Etruscan helmet; she had been told about it when she was very young, and was sure that it was already in the house by about 1918. But it had not been kept in the drawing room - it sat on a table in the Stone Hall, together with a narwhale horn and a scold's bridle. It might well have acquired its loose label from another object that really did have a local provenance. The helmet does not bear witness to a foreign warrior in Britain in the fourth century BC, but it is a genuine antiquity and a rare example of its type. It was not a recent illegal import because it had been in the family since 1918, so it could be bought and sold quite legally in the antiquities market. The British Museum purchased it.

The Wallingford brooches and the Watney helmet acquired their false provenances in all innocence, but in the case of the Suffolk helmet there was deliberate deception. In 1978 the dealer David Miller (another who dealt in Salisbury Hoard antiquities) submitted photographs of an Iron Age bronze helmet that he was selling on behalf of a continental dealer. It had a vague provenance — 'found in Suffolk' — so I asked him to bring it in for examination. It was surely a genuine antiquity, but the provenance seemed most unlikely. The British Museum Research Laboratory carried out authenticity tests and I wrote to Ulrich Schaaff, in Mainz, the foremost authority on Celtic helmets. The Research Laboratory agreed that the helmet seemed genuine, and were able to go some way towards destroying the Suffolk provenance, suggesting that it had been buried in a fairly dry tomb. Schaaff went even further: he knew the helmet, which had been offered to the Museum at Mainz by a German dealer called Waldner. At that time it had a German provenance - 'Bavaria'! But another German dealer told Schaaff that it had been taken to Munich by a Turkish *Gastarbeiter*: it had been found in Turkey, and had been exported illegally.

David Miller confirmed that Waldner was the continental dealer who owned the helmet, and he confronted him with the story that Schaaff had told me. Waldner agreed that he had offered the helmet to Schaaff, and admitted that he had invented the Bavarian provenance so that it would be more interesting to the German museum. But he claimed to know nothing about the Turkish *Gastarbeiter*. Indeed, he said that he had bought the helmet from a Liverpool man, and he provided Miller with the address and telephone number. Miller persevered, phoned the man, a Mr Poland, and asked for an account of the provenance in writing. This is Mr

Poland's story: 'Whilst on holiday touring the South of England roughly 6 years ago, I came across a lorry which had run out of fuel, the driver asked for my assistance in helping him, at which time I drove him to the nearest garage at hand for fuel and back to where his lorry was parked. To repay me for the help I had given him, as he was short of cash, he gave me a few articles he had picked up with his load.

'On returning from my trip, I gave the sword and helmet to my sister, the sword she sold to a market in Liverpool. The helmet she took back to Germany and sold to a shop in Munich and the one last article I am enclosing and hope it will be of value to you.' This one last article was the cheek-piece of another helmet, which Miller subsequently sold to Robert Erskine.

We hear of some interesting provenances, but we rarely see objects that have fallen off the back of a lorry. Needless to say, the helmet was returned to David Miller and doubtless he returned it to Waldner. I wonder where it is now, and where its present owner thinks it was found.

The problems concerning the veracity of provenances have increased vastly in recent years with the advent of the metal detector, which accounts for the discovery of huge numbers of ancient metal artefacts. Treasure hunting is now a popular hobby and every weekend thousands of devotees take to the field. Most of their finds are of limited archaeological interest, but inevitably a few are significant. The archaeologist would like to record those significant finds, and perhaps a museum would like to acquire them, but that is not always possible. Apart from some items of gold or silver and associated pieces, and finds from scheduled ancient monuments, antiquities in British soil are afforded no protection by the law. They belong to the landowner, and he can do what he likes with them. The treasure hunter wanting to search a field must ask the permission of the landowner and most will then make a formal agreement, usually to the effect that the finder will declare all his finds and anything of value will be shared between them. Some landowners say that they are not interested in items of base metal, but they do want to know about any discoveries of gold or silver. The vast majority of metal detectorists operate according to a Code of Conduct published by the National Council for Metal Detecting. Some of them show their finds to museums or professional archaeologists who provide a free identification service in return for the opportunity to record artefacts of real interest. And some of the more enlightened metal detectorists will donate their finds to a museum.

John Weeks is a good example of the enlightened metal detectorist. He lives at Foxton, near Cambridge, and for several years has used his metal detector in local fields. He runs a society, the Foxton Forum, and occasionally lectures to other societies in the area. A few years ago he brought some of his finds to the British Museum for identification, and among them was a piece that caught my eye. It was an unfinished Roman brooch: a brooch that had been discarded at a very early stage in its manufacture, when it looked nothing like a brooch. I recognised it because similar unfinished brooches had been found on one of my excavations — indeed, John Weeks' site at Foxton was only the second place in the country to produce them. He generously donated his find, and over the next couple of years he found and donated three more. They are not attractive artefacts, and they have no monetary value: no dealer would give them a second glance and most metal detectorists would probably discard them. But they help to show how brooches were made, they will be useful to researchers present and future, and they allow us to identify a site where Roman brooches were manufactured.

If the archaeologist has direct contact with a metal detectorist it is usually possible to record an artefact and to establish its precise provenance. Occasionally there are problems, especially if the treasure hunter is claiming title to an artefact that he has stolen: then we may get a fake provenance. Only the finder knows the true provenance, and only in very rare instances can it be verified independently.

Just occasionally, even a direct contact fails to produce a precise provenance. In September 1993 a metal detectorist submitted a remarkable bronze artefact **(Colour plate 20)**. It was small, 110mm ($4\frac{1}{4}$in) long, with a hooked blade at one end and a flat handle beautifully decorated on both sides. I had never seen anything like it. The decoration was distinctive, definitely British, probably third century BC, but at that time blades were made of iron, not bronze. Where was it found? In a field that had been harvested, the harvesters were still working there when it was found, in the vicinity of Daneswick, in Hertfordshire. I explained that that was not good enough: I had to know the precise spot, and as the finder wanted to sell it I needed to know that he had good title. His agreement with the farmer allowed him to keep any bronze finds, but gold and silver had to be shared. A fairly common arrangement. And as he was a reputable metal detectorist, a club official, I believed him. But he refused to identify the precise provenance. Why? Because he had given his word to the farmer, who was determined not to be troubled by archaeologists! More commonly metal detectorists refuse to reveal a good site to archaeologists, or indeed to other metal detectorists, because they think that there might still be rich pickings in the future.

Some metal detectorists look to their hobby as a means of making money, so they would usually bypass the museum and go direct to a dealer or auction house. This might be the most convenient solution if a metal detectorist finds an artefact of value and has an agreement to split the proceeds with the farmer. Museums are always short of money and are hard pressed to purchase artefacts; indeed, some museums refuse to have anything to do with discoveries made by metal detectorists. But there is a network of antiquities dealers across the country, and for the more valuable antiquities there are auction houses. Many antiquities disappear into the trade every year, and usually their provenance is then lost. The museums, scholarship and the public are the losers. Even if an artefact is ultimately acquired by a museum it is very rare indeed to be able to recover a reliable provenance. Once an antiquity has been removed from the earth it is virtually impossible to re-identify the spot where it was found.

But the metal detectorist who has the landowner's permission to sell a find is behaving legally; he is experiencing the thrill of discovery and making a small amount of profit out of it. Only occasionally does illegality enter the field. The metal detectorist might be tempted to conceal his find from the farmer. Suppose he has spent the day in the field, collected a bagful of rubbish — and one rather fine Roman brooch. Who's to know if the farmer is shown the rubbish, and the detectorist pockets the brooch? That does happen, and in such cirmcumstances the brooch certainly loses its provenance or acquires a false provenance.

Most of the finds discovered by metal detectorists are corroded pieces of iron, and bronze or brass is the best that they can hope for, but just occasionally they strike gold or silver. Then they must report their find not only to the landowner, but to the local Coroner, via the police or a museum. This is a provision of the 1996 Treasure Act; previously it was part of Treasure Trove regulations. In England such pieces are submitted initially to the British Museum where they are identified and their metal content is assessed. Then the local coroner holds an inquest to determine whether or not they are 'treasure' and to confirm the identity of the finder. If a museum wishes to acquire antiquities thus declared 'treasure' it must finance a reward which is paid to the finder.

Finders of 'treasure' are rewarded in an attempt to encourage them to declare their discoveries, and in many cases it has the desired effect. But we have no idea how many gold and silver antiquities go undeclared. If coins are taken as a guideline then there could be a considerable undisclosed element. Every year coins are found in their thousands and they circulate readily between collectors and dealers. For the Iron Age, issues can be linked to local tribes, and new batches of coins on the market usually mean that a hoard has been found in that particular part of the country. On this basis it was estimated in 1994 that of 6600 coins from hoards found by metal detectorists in the tribal area of the Iceni (essentially Norfolk) since 1970, only 330 were declared for the purposes of Treasure Trove. And Norfolk has an excellent record for cooperation between archaeologists and metal detectorists. Other antiquities are much rarer than coins, and we have no comparable figures, but we do occasionally hear whispers. There was a persistent rumour that a gold torque (neck-ring) from the great hoard site at Snettisham was discovered and quietly removed in the 1970s. Local archaeologists heard of another torque from Narford, not far from Snettisham, almost certainly from a hoard. The trail led to, and stopped at, a London dealer who doubtless sold it abroad. But we had no more than a rumour to go on, no photograph or drawing of the torque ever reached the archaeological world. In 1991 Paul Robinson, Curator of Devizes Museum, was told that two gold torques had been found and sold to a dealer within a week. More recently, Tony Rook heard of a silver torque and gold coins from a site in Hertfordshire. They were found by night-hawks and sold to the trade the following day.

We were more fortunate in another case involving a gold torque found in Norfolk, when detective work by police and archaeologists led to the recovery of an archaeological provenance.

The torque in question was quite similar in form and date to those found at Snettisham, but before deposition in antiquity it had been treated in a curious way. The two terminals had been detached, and the strands that had linked them had been cut into many small pieces. The initial discovery was of the terminals, which look like a pair of thick discs, each finely decorated on one face **(Colour plate 19)**. They were found by Geoffrey Peach in 1984. This was long before the Treasure Act, when discoveries of gold and silver were dealt with under the ancient concept of Treasure Trove. Peach should have declared the find to the farmer but he decided to keep it for himself; by selling privately he thought that he would circumvent the Treasure Trove proceedings. So he took his find to Sotheby's and was advised to submit it for one of their antiquities auctions.

News of the decorated terminals soon reached the late Tony Gregory, one of Norfolk's greatest archaeologists and a pioneer in fostering good relations between metal detectorists and archaeologists. Tony passed the word to me in February 1985; Sotheby's confirmed that the terminals were with them, and agreed to lend them to the British Museum for study and identification. It was obvious that they were made of gold — or a gold/silver alloy — and there was every reason to suppose that they were a recent discovery, so the Coroner was informed and the find was seized on his behalf. That brought a furious response from the auctioneers, and prompted an irate telephone call from the finder who demanded the immediate return of his property. Peach argued that the terminals were not subject to the law of Treasure Trove because they were made of base metal, and they had not been found in the ground: they had been discovered under the floor-boards in the attic of a house owned by his brother, at Fincham, Norfolk. But he was mistaken about the composition of the metal, and the circumstances of discovery did not affect the issue. To be considered for Treasure Trove, items of gold or silver had to have been concealed, not necessarily in the ground, by a person unknown. As Peach did not know who had concealed them in the attic he was advised to contact the Coroner. It would have been a remarkable coincidence for a known metal detectorist to find the terminals of an Iron Age gold torque in the attic of his brother's house.

H.M.Coroner for the Lynn District of Norfolk, Bill Knowles, held an inquest in September 1985. It was alleged that Peach had claimed to have found the terminals 'near Fakenham', but his evidence to the Coroner maintained that they had been found in the house at Fincham in August 1984. The jury returned a verdict of Treasure Trove, but they had no faith in Peach's evidence and declared that the find had been made at a place unknown. The terminals were valued at £25,000 by the British Museum, and that valuation was approved by the Treasure Trove Reviewing Committee (then run by the Treasury). Under normal circumstances a reward amounting to the full valuation would be paid to the finder, but in this case the Treasury took into account the attempt to conceal the discovery and awarded an ex gratia payment of one-tenth of the market value. The British Museum paid the reward and acquired the two terminals: one was placed on permanent display and the other went on loan to the Norwich Castle Museum.

Almost two years later, in 1987, Stephen Brown was using a metal detector in a field at Bawsey, Norfolk, when he discovered two twisted strands of gold wire from a torque. Subsequently Peach, in conversation with Tony Gregory and his colleague Andrew Rogerson, admitted that the torque terminals had also been found at Bawsey, and he marked the find-spot on a map. The Norfolk police took an interest in the matter and asked the Oxford metallurgist and archaeologist, Peter Northover, to carry out metal analyses of the terminals and the wire strands. Northover concluded that there was a strong possibility that they all belonged to the one artefact. Further metal detecting was obstructed because someone deliberately scattered aluminium fragments over a large area of the field.

Peach was charged with perjury and theft, and the case occupied ten days in May and June 1989, at Norwich Crown Court before His Honour Judge John Blofeld. The defence brought witnesses from Liverpool University to contest the metallurgical evidence and to present soil analyses, but the judge advised the jury to ignore the scientific evidence because it dealt with possibilities; the case rested on conversations between Peach and the Norfok archaeologists. The defence alleged that Peach was the victim of a conspiracy between Gregory, Rogerson and the metal detectorist Brown, but the jury was not convinced. Peach was convicted and sentenced to 15 months' imprisonment (six of them suspended).

10. Context

All antiquities found by metal detectorists have a provenance, even if it is rapidly lost, but few of them have a context. Most have been disturbed, usually by ploughing, from the place in which they were originally deposited, and any other antiquities once associated with them will have been dispersed. But if the metal detectorist is lucky enough to find a hoard or a grave, a skeleton or cremation accompanied by artefacts, then those artefacts do have a context. Everything in a hoard or grave was buried together at the same time; the arrangement and association of pieces might help to explain the function of some of the artefacts, give a reason for their deposition, and provide useful evidence of date. It might be possible to date some of the artefacts quite closely, and they in turn can be used to date the others. Context provides a date for deposition, in that all the artefacts were deposited on one occasion; it does not provide a date for manufacture, because some of the artefacts could have been made earlier than others (as in the Salisbury Hoard). But the construction of a series of securely associated artefacts, especially from hoards and graves, provides the best chronology for which an archaeologist can hope.

If a metal detectorist does find associated artefacts it is vital that they are properly recorded and kept together so that future generations of scholars can study them. In the Iron Age graves are far more common than hoards so they are the most likely context in which associated artefacts will be found. It is unlikely that the metal detectorist will be looking for a grave specifically, and it is unlikely that he has ever come across one before, so he is ill-prepared to tackle a task that might well become very complicated. Furthermore, because the metal detector has limited penetration, it will locate artefacts only in shallow graves and especially in graves that have been disturbed by ploughing. Such graves present a challenge to the most experienced excavator, and the average treasure hunter would probably remove the metal artefacts without realising that he was dealing with a grave. But there are exceptions.

Justin Hayes and Gordon Barker were searching a field at Elsenham, Essex, in September 1990 when they discovered first a group of metal objects and then some broken pots. They showed their find to the farmer who arranged for an archaeologist to see it: they had uncovered a Roman cremation burial. The cremated bones had probably been in a glass vessel, but that and other finds had been damaged by ploughing and by the cutting of a field-drain some time before the metal detectorists arrived on the scene. Their outstanding find was a small hexagonal bronze box decorated with fine millefiori enamel in six colours **(Colour plate 21)**. It is a rare type, with only another dozen known from the Roman Empire. The Elsenham box was the first to be found in Britain, and the only one from the entire Empire that could be dated by association with other artefacts. The other finds included the remains of six pots, a bronze lock-plate and key from a wooden box, an iron lamp, 12 bone and 6 glass game counters, a unique bronze cup and three silver coins. The burial must have taken place after the date of the latest coin (circa AD 145–148).

Having excavated the grave to the best of their ability, the metal detectorists allowed the County Archaeological Unit to examine and record all their finds, and then published a report on their work (in the metal detectorist's magazine, *The Searcher*) with a promptitude that puts some archaeologists to shame. It was quite obvious that they had made an important find so they decided to sell it. They had a 50:50 agreement with the landowner, so jointly they had a legal title to the finds, and they wanted to upgrade their metal detectors. So they took a day off work and went up to Christie's to seek a valuation. That was where the trouble started.

'The young lady was most helpful, though sorry to have to tell us that as far as auctions go there is no sale for complete contents of Roman graves .... But the enamelled pot did interest her .... "Special", she said it was, and "very collectable".' So an important and fairly rich Roman grave-group, quite well-excavated and reasonably recorded, was to be split by the auctioneers. Christie's wanted to sell the enamelled box for a high price, but they had no interest at all in the fate of the other artefacts. The box duly appeared as lot 129 in Christie's Antiquities Sale on 10 July 1991, without a provenance and with no mention of associated finds. The estimate was £6000 - £9000, but in fact it sold for £33,000 and the purchaser applied for an Export Licence to take it abroad. Fortunately there is a happy ending to the story, because the export of the box was halted under regulations controlling the export from Britain of antiquities and works of art. Time was allowed for a British buyer to raise the purchase price and the British Museum Society came to the rescue. They presented the box to the Museum in commemoration of Sir David Wilson's directorship (1977-92). The metal detectorists generously donated the other artefacts, so the entire grave-group could be kept together. Another piece of our heritage preserved, but with no thanks to the auctioneers.

In the spring of 1993 Darren Nichols and his girl friend Michelle O'Rorke discovered a decorated bronze mirror and a bronze brooch in the grounds of Chilham Castle, Kent **(Fig 13)**. They were newcomers to the hobby of metal detecting and did not know what to do: at the time Darren was unwell, which complicated the issue. Eventually they showed their find to archaeologists at the Canterbury Archaeological Trust, and subsequently to Canterbury Museum, but they seem to have been deeply suspicious of such 'official' contacts. However, they were persuaded to reveal their find to the landowner, Annabelle Viscountess Massereene and Ferrard, and the two parties agreed to share it. Keith Parfitt, an archaeologist with the Canterbury Archaeological Trust, worked hard to win Darren's confidence, and eventually, in July 1994, more than a year after the mirror had been found, he was shown the precise site of the discovery. Lady Massereene gave permission for an archaeological excavation, and the remains of a shallow grave were unearthed, with cremated bones, a pot and the pair to the brooch that the metal detectorists had found.

Darren Nicholls was unwilling to donate his find to a museum, but he did show it to Ken Reedie, curator of Canterbury Museum, and he took Reedie's advice and submitted it to the British Museum for study. The metal detectorists wanted to sell it for the best price they could get. They had already consulted Sotheby's, who suggested a reserve of £3000, but an unnamed dealer had indicated that £60,000 — £70,000 was nearer the mark — although he had not seen the mirror, and as far as I could gather he had not even seen a photograph of it. As Iron Age mirrors go, it was surprisingly crude, but its presence in a grave-group gave it great archaeological interest. I thought that Sotheby's reserve was on the low side and advised the metal detectorists to ask Peter Clayton, of Seaby's, for a second opinion. Peter suggested £4000 – £6000 for the three pieces of bronze

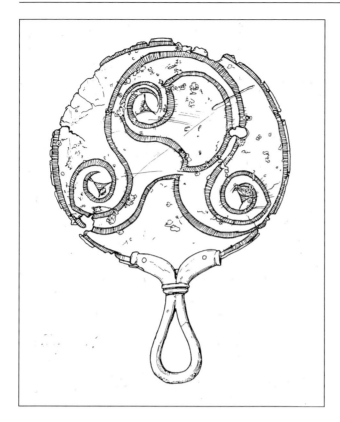

13 The decorated back of a bronze mirror from Chilham Castle (scale $\frac{1}{2}$). Drawn by Jo Bacon.

and it seemed to me that he had hit the right level. After speaking to Ken Reedie I asked the metal detectorists to sell the entire grave-group to the Canterbury Museum or the British Museum, on the basis of Peter Clayton's estimate. But meanwhile Sotheby's had written to them and raised their reserve to £10,000, so they decided to submit their finds for public auction.

After the Elsenham experience I was worried that the grave-group would not be kept intact, so I explained the problem in a letter to Lady Massereene. She assured me that the intention was to sell the entire grave-group. That would have created a very interesting precedent: the first time that cremated human bones would have been sold at public auction. But when we received the catalogue for Sotheby's July sale of antiquities only the mirror and the two brooches were listed, lot no 3, with an estimate of £6000 – £9000, the property of Darren Nichols, Esq. I wrote to Lady Massereene. Was Nichols indeed the owner, and where was the rest of the grave-group, the pottery and cremated bones? She responded by phone and then by letter: she and Nichols were joint owners and the pottery and bones would go to the museum that purchased lot 3. With the support of the British Museum, Canterbury Museum successfully applied to the Victoria and Albert Museum for a grant towards the purchase at auction, and set a realistic limit higher than the estimate. In the event they were the underbidders.

We made every effort to locate the new owner of the Chilham Castle mirror and brooches, because other scholars would need to examine such important finds. Ken Reedie spoke to Sotheby's and sent them a letter to forward to the purchaser, but it produced no result. We were confident that no other museum in Britain would have bid for them, but there was always a possibility that they had gone abroad. In that case we would have to await an application for an export licence. They could have been purchased by a British collector, of course, though for antiquities of that value the field was limited. One possibility was Robin Symes, the West End antiquities dealer and collector who had handled some of the Salisbury Hoard antiquities. I came across his name first when he purchased a unique deer figurine for an extremely high price in the 1970s. Allegedly it was Celtic, and from Leintwardine in Shropshire. Subsequently we were shown some crude immitations of it and borrowed the object itself for comparison. We never did sort out the fakes, but there was no reason to doubt that Symes' figure was a genuine antiquity. Reedie contacted Symes' office and I raised the matter with a member of his staff who called in at the museum one day, but nobody seemed to know anything about antiquities from Chilham Castle. There the matter had to rest for several months.

About this time two other decorated mirrors were found by metal detectorists, which is curious, because they are not very common. One of them, from Portesham, Dorset, was being researched by Andrew Fitzpatrick, of Wessex Archaeology, who was keen to examine comparable mirrors. He had heard about the Chilham Castle find and wanted to see it. The British Museum could not help, beyond suggesting that he should write to Sotheby's, which he did. And Fitzpatrick succeeded where Reedie and I had failed. The Chilham Castle mirror had indeed been purchased by Robin Symes, acting on behalf of an anonymous collector. The collector was willing to let scholars examine it, but not in the British Museum. It was delivered to Robin Symes' showrooms, just off Piccadilly, where it was examined by Fitzpatrick and me, and an illustrator made an accurate record of it. The mirror was then returned to the anonymous collector.

The Chilham Castle mirror is not a major work of art. Its simple design has been quite crudely executed. But it is the only decorated Iron Age mirror to have been found in Kent, and it can be dated better than most mirrors because it was associated with other artefacts in a grave-group. Its place in the story of Kent is quite significant, but the people of Kent (and beyond) cannot see it and it is not too easy for scholars to study it. Perhaps one day the anonymous collector will give it to Canterbury Museum, where it can re-join the burial urn and cremation donated by Lady Massereene.

It is quite possible for a context to be destroyed in all innocence. George Wallace is a keen metal detectorist who shares his hobby with three friends. They make formal written agreements with landowners and work together as a group. One Saturday in October 1992 George, unusually, was alone and he decided to detect on one of their regular sites in fields at Essendon, Hertfordshire. But that day there was a shoot, and George could not work his favourite patch, so he turned to a hillside that he had previously ignored. Almost immediately he got a good signal and found a gold coin; and more gold followed. The following morning he returned to the site with his friends, and the four of them worked their gold mine for several days. When the finds eventually petered out they reported the discovery to the Coroner and the Hertfordshire Archaeological Trust, who informed the British Museum. They had found 69 gold coins, as well as a couple of gold ingots, some gold sheet and the remains of a torque. Different from the torque found at Bawsey, it had large hollow globular terminals linked not by strands of wire but by a hollow tube. It had been broken and scattered by the plough, and the two terminals were about 20m (65ft) apart. Inside one terminal were several pieces of folded gold sheet and six or eight coins. The finders tipped out the contents, unfolding one of the pieces of sheet, and carefully packed the coins with all the others from the site. Never before had a tubular torque been associated with coins: the four metal detectorists had found the two types in a context, a unique association that provided invaluable evidence for the date of the torque. They had taken very good care of the artefacts, but totally destroyed this really important piece of evidence. They could not remember which of the coins had been found in the terminal of the torque.

When the British Museum team came to examine the field more coins and fragments of gold were found, but everything was in the plough-soil: no nucleus of a hoard survived. The gold finds were scattered but two marked concentrations 30m apart indicated the sites of two different hoards, and the chronology and typology of the coins suggested that originally there might have been other deposits buried at intervals over about 150 years (say, 100 BC to AD 50). If the coins from the torque terminal had been separately packed they would have provided a close date for the torque; as it is, we have to be content with a range between 100 BC and AD 50. But George and his colleagues had properly declared their finds, and following a Treasure Trove inquest at Hertford they received a reward amounting to the full market value, which they shared with the farmer according to their agreement.

The finest hoards of Iron Age gold torques that have ever been discovered came to light through the efforts of one of the best of metal detectorists. Cecil (Charles) Hodder lives near Kings Lynn; he retired a while ago and spends a lot of time with his metal detector. He served with the RAF during the last war, is upright and honest, full of energy and dogged perseverance, and he has a happy knack of discovering unusual antiquities. He does not sign agreements with farmers, but shows them all that he finds and is usually allowed to keep everything. Several museums have benefited from his generosity, and over the years he has established a good working relationship with the Norfolk Archaeological Unit, who record any of his finds that interest them. In 1989 Charles Hodder was given permission to detect in the 'Gold Field' at Snettisham, a field so called because hoards of gold torques and coins had been found there about 40 years previously. In 1989 he found a few oddments, which were duly recorded by the Norfolk archaeologists, and then, the next year, he really did strike gold. Following a fairly promising signal from his detector he dug a small hole and found a length of thick gold wire. Checking the bottom of the hole he got a much louder signal and unearthed a mass of gold **(Colour plate 22)**. Charles fully appreciated the importance of his find, and realised that it should be unearthed by archaeologists. But it was the Saturday of the Bank Holiday week-end, and his archaeological contacts were away. He could not leave the treasure in the field over the week-end, so he excavated it himself. The landowner was also away, so Charles took his treasure home. His wife did not share his passion for antiquities and would not have a hoard of dirty metal in the house, so more than 9 kilos of ancient gold and silver spent the weekend in the garage. Then in rapid succession the Norfolk Archaeological Unit, the landowner and the Coroner were informed of the discovery, and the hoard was delivered to the British Museum for study. In due course the Coroner held an inquest and the hoard was declared Treasure

Trove: Charles received a substantial reward, amounting to the full market value of his find.

But that was not the end of the Snettisham story. The British Museum decided to investigate the site to see if any more hoards had survived and to try to establish why hoards had been buried in that particular spot. Charles Hodder accepted an invitation to join us, and like all the other members of the team he signed a disclaimer to the effect that he would not expect a reward for any discovery that he might make. Treasure Trove rewards are paid in order to encourage members of the public to declare their finds; archaeologists do not need this incentive. In the course of five weeks five more hoards of gold torques were carefully excavated and recorded: Charles found three of them and my colleague Tony Pacitto found the other two. For the first time ever archaeologists had accurately recorded hoards of Iron Age gold torques in the field **(Colour plate 23)**. Over the next three years these hoards were appreciated by thousands of people at special exhibitions in Norwich, London and Cardiff, and they are now on permanent display at the British Museum.

But the Snettisham excavation was not a treasure hunt. At least 11 and perhaps as many as 13 hoards had been found over the years, so this was the ideal site to investigate the reasons for the deposition of Iron Age hoards. Over two seasons we searched a vast area of plough-soil for traces of hoards and thoroughly stripped an area of about a quarter of an acre towards the centre of the distribution. But in that area we found not a hint of any building, boundary or pit contemporary with the deposits of gold. It seemed that the hoards had been buried in open country well away from any settlement. In our second and third seasons we cast the net over a wider area and identified an impressive ditch that defined a huge polygonal enclosure (about 20 acres) with the hoards more or less in the middle. The ditch had sufficient pottery in its filling to allow us to date it with confidence: it had been open towards the end of the first century AD, and then it had been allowed to silt and become overgrown. The hoards that we had found, and those found previously, might well have been buried within a year or two of one another. Those that could be dated accurately ended with coins of about 70 BC, and there was no clear sign that the other hoards were significantly earlier or later. There were some later coins, dating about 50 BC, but after that the extensive excavations produced nothing until the big ditch started silting at the end of the first century AD. Of course the ditch could have been dug much earlier, and regularly cleaned, but if that was so the people who maintained it left nothing within the area of our excavations. There was no evidence for activity on the site for about 150 years; the hoards and the ditched enclosure could have been two unrelated features several generations apart.

Some time after our last season at Snettisham it became apparent that one hoard had got away — and a very significant hoard it was, too. When we arrived on site in 1991 the farm manager told us that the gamekeeper and the woodman had disturbed 'night-hawks' (illicit metal detectorists) working in the Gold Field just to the north of our previous excavations. We examined the area and found it littered with fragments of cut metal sheet — a standard ploy used to deter other metal detectorists. There was also evidence of an excavation — an excavation that had uncovered a considerable amount of iron slag. We explored further and found that the slag had come from the filling of the big enclosure ditch: someone had cut a huge hole into it quite recently — at the bottom we found sugar-beet from the crop that had only just been removed. It seemed that the night-hawks had detected the slag, and wasted a great deal of effort digging it out. Throughout our excavations warders from the British Museum mounted a 24-hour guard and the night-hawks never returned.

A few months later I heard rumours that a coin hoard had been removed from the Gold Field about the time of our 1991 excavation. The informant had commented that our security had been inadequate, but I was quite confident that it had not been breached. I was told that I might get more information from Wobbly Dave who lived in Essex, drove a blue Cortina, and always had a pick-axe handle at the ready. He had earned his nickname because he would throw a wobbly if he was crossed. But my informant did not know how I could make contact, so sadly I was spared the experience. At that time I thought that the hoard, if there was a hoard, had probably come from another site.

But I had to think again about 18 months later, in October 1993, when I was given some very precise information. The hoard had comprised 6000 coins, and most of them had been to the USA and back. They had been found by a metal detectorist who had been looking for a torque, and he had been most disappointed with his 6000 coins! The site was described precisely, by the track, adjoining the wood, half-way down the field. Most of the coins were silver, and they had been buried in a silver bowl; below it, as a separate deposit, were 500 gold coins and some curious ingots. My informant's description of the ingots matched exactly the unique ingots found at

Essendon. Very few people knew about the Essendon ingots: this story sounded genuine. More impressive still was the mention of a silver bowl, which would have been extremely rare in the context of a Celtic coin hoard. In 1991 when we were working in the area previously covered by our 1990 spoil-heap, an area bordering the distribution of night-hawk decoy fragments and by the track, adjoining the wood, half-way down the field, we found several fragments from the rim of a silver bowl. This was no coincidence: as well as digging into the iron slag, the night-hawks had found a hoard.

The Bowl Hoard was illegally excavated, stolen and dispersed though dealers. It was not declared for Treasure Trove. But it is now well-known to scholars interested in Celtic coins, and many of its components have been catalogued. It is said that the silver bowl survives, and it is still in England. It is infuriating to have lost evidence from an archaeological site, especially from a site on which a considerable amount of public money had been expended. It would be bad enough if the lost hoard merely duplicated the evidence from the others, but it does not. It is quite different. The Bowl Hoard had coins that ranged from about 30 BC to AD 40: it belongs to the blank period between the main series of hoards and the time that the ditch started to silt. It has a significant bearing on our interpretation of the site. But what is its status academically? How reliable is the information about this hoard, and can it really be acknowledged as evidence? What is the use of rumours that cannot be substantiated?

Provenance and context should be carefully recorded by all finders, casual finders and metal detectorists as well as archaeologists. Collectors, dealers and auction houses should encourage the practice and make the effort to keep this information with every artefact. Unlike postage stamps, postcards, bus tickets and other collectables, antiquities are unique and each one can make a small contribution to human history.

11. Protection

British antiquities can be discovered, excavated, sold and even exported without the authorities being any the wiser. but there is no means of assessing the scale of the problem objectively. The losers are scholars and interested members of the public, present and future, quite apart from the landowners who had a rightful title to the finds.

In order to illustrate the problem perhaps we should organise an exhibition of Treasure — British Treasure — found with the aid of metal detectors. The metal detecting press frequently proclaims the success of their fraternity as opposed to the efforts of archaeologists, and when it comes to 'treasure' they are correct. There is no better way to find 'treasure' than by using a metal detector. In our exhibition we could show some of the major hoards discovered in recent times — the Thetford Treasure (1979), the Hoxne Hoard (1992), Snettisham Hoards F–L (1990). It would be a fantastic display. But I would reserve a case for the Icklingham Bronzes (1982), an amazing hoard that was dispersed abroad. American collectors might be persuaded to lend some of it, but inevitably there would be empty spaces because the present location of some pieces is unknown. And the label would have to explain that we cannot prove that it came from Icklingham, though it was certainly circulating in Suffolk and it is probably British. The Snettisham Bowl Hoard (1991), perhaps the most important hoard of British coins found this century, would also deserve a case to itself — an empty case. We could show 1041 coins from the Wanborough Hoard (1983/4) leaving spaces for at least 9000 more (some estimates put the overall total above 20,000). The Salisbury Hoard (1985) would have to be there, filling two-thirds of a very large case: the other third would be conspicuously empty.

Such a display would have visual impact, and would give some indication of what we have lost in the very recent past. It could never be complete, because nobody is aware of the full extent of our loss: doubtless there are other spectacular hoards, especially coin hoards, and certainly there are many hundreds, nay, thousands, of individual artefacts.

Whilst to some extent the loss of antiquities can be demonstrated in an exhibition, the equally significant loss of knowledge is much harder to appreciate. The Salisbury Hoard provides a good example because beyond the antiquities is the remarkable phenomenon that they represent: the collection of antiquities by ancient Britons, a practice hitherto unappreciated. That phenomenon will now feature in all future books on British prehistory and in many future books on primitive religions. The discovery of the Salisbury Hoard has shed a flicker of light on an obscure corner of man's past: light that could have been extinguished as readily as the artefacts were dispersed.

Some of our antiquities do have legal protection. Until recently England's nearest approach to an antiquities law was the medieval concept of Treasure Trove, a prerogative right of the Crown established before the twelfth century, subsequently pressed into service as a make-shift means of protecting antiquities. In the past if a deposit of gold or silver artefacts, bullion or coins was discovered, and if the owner could not be traced but could reasonably be assumed to have intended to recover his property, then the find was declared Treeasure Trove and seized for the Crown. Over the years the Crown occasionally donated the right of Treasure Trove in certain localities to various nobles and others, including church dignitaries. Franchisees included the Duchies of Cornwall and Lancaster as well as the Sees of Canterbury, York, Durham, Salisbury and Worcester, and the cities of London and Bristol. Today some retain their rights: the Duchy of Lancaster, for instance, owned the Snettisham Treasure. But the Sovereign's right was surrendered in return for the Civil List and Treasure Trove seized in the name of the Queen was then taken by the State.

In September 1997 the Treasure Act came into operation. Based on the old Treasure Trove concept, the new act removed the need to establish that objects were hidden with the intention of being recovered; it defined the precious metal content required for a find to qualify as treasure; and it extended protection to other objects found in archaeological association with finds of treasure. One of the key principles of the Treasure Act, as with the recent operation of Treasure Trove, is that finders should receive an *ex gratia* reward for reporting the discovery of treasure to the authorities. Not a nominal reward, but a reward amounting to the full market value of the find. And there could be no fairer way of assessing that market value: valuation is assessed by an independent reviewing committee appointed by the Department of Culture, Media and Sport, including both scholars and representatives of dealers and auction houses.

The Treasure Act is an important step forward, but it still applies essentially to objects of gold and silver, which represent a very small percentage of archaeological finds. The Salisbury Hoard, for instance, composed entirely of bronzes, falls outside its scope.

The only other legal protection afforded to antiquities is provided by the Import, Export and Customs Powers (Defence) Act of 1939. Under these regulations every antiquity found on British soil requires a licence before it can be legally exported (coins worth less than £35,000 are excluded). The licence is issued by the Export Licensing Unit of the Department of Culture, Media and Sport, on the advice of the appropriate keeper at the British Museum. This system can be effective when dealing with some valuable antiquities, as the Elsenham case shows (p. 140), but others escape the net. Thus the Icklingham bronzes were exported without licences, and once such antiquities are abroad there is very little that the authorities can do. The export licence regulations apply to all antiquities regardless of value (apart from coins) but it seems to be easy to evade them. Many antiquities from the Salisbury Hoard were exported (see the chart, **Fig.6**) and each one required a licence, but not a single application was made.

In England all antiquities not covered by the Treasure Act belong to the owner of the land. And in an ideal world landowner, metal detectorist and archaeologist could work together comfortably. The discovery of the Salisbury Hoard, for instance, could have had a different scenario: Two metal detectorists, James Garriock and Terry Rossiter, want to search for Roman coins, so they contact a farmer, Reginald Cook, and the three of them sign an agreement as approved by the National Council for Metal Detecting. Instead of Roman coins they find the most incredible hoard of Bronze Age artefacts. Immediately they contact Andrew Lawson, Director of Wessex Archaeology, and he arranges for it to be carefully excavated and recorded by archaeologists. David Keys hears about it almost as soon as Andrew, and *The Independent* carries a full-page article including photographs of Garriock and Rossiter. The press treats them as local heroes, who have discovered 'the find of the century'. Peter Clayton values the hoard, and the British Museum purchases it with the aid of a grant from the National Heritage Memorial Fund. Mr Cook honours his agreement with the metal detectorists, who receive more than £20,000 each. Would that it had happened that way! Garriock and Rossiter would have been richer and a lot happier. The archaeological world would have had full details, and the public would have been able to see the entire hoard.

But it didn't happen that way. Instead of involving the archaeologists the metal detectorists preferred to go to a dealer. They told John Cummings that they had title to the find, and he believed them. The situation could have been retrieved if he had pursued the matter more thoroughly and insisted on talking to the owner of the land. But he didn't, and of course he was under no obligation to do so. The trial judge ruled that he was entitled to believe what he was told. Perhaps it would have been another matter if Cummings had realised the full significance of the find, but he was at the beginning of his career as a dealer and he did not appreciate its true worth to archaeology.

Doubtless most other antiquities dealers would have behaved like Cummings. When the 'Batheaston' Hoard was taken to Sotheby's what enquiries were made? Presumably they asked the vendor if he had title; he lied; they sold the antiquities. In another context a Sotheby's official was quoted as saying 'I don't think one ever knows where antiquities come from', and 'We assume that our clients have title to whatever it is they are selling'. By luck the 'Batheaston' Hoard remained in one lot, and was bought by the British Museum: it could so easily have been bought by the trade, split and dispersed, and another unique hoard would have been lost to archaeology. As it is, we cannot be absolutely sure that the 'Batheaston' bronzes belonged to a single hoard, and we do not know where they were found. We have identified the finders, but what is the good of that?

Antiquities dealers purchase from honest vendors, who really do have title to antiquities. They purchase from vendors who are essentially honest, like Garriock and Rossiter, but who succumb to the one-off lie in exceptional circumstances. And they purchase from night-hawks, the criminals of the metal detecting world.

Night-hawks are a menace, but it seems that there is little that can be done about them. Recently three of them appeared in a television documentary, openly boasting about their activities. They work by night and search fields, ancient monuments, and even archaeological sites in the the course of excavation. Their hallmark is the overnight appearance of small pits, sometimes large pits. They sell their antiquities to dealers who believe that they have genuine title to them. There are stories that they offer physical violence (as in the case of Wobbly Dave, p. 147), and some are said to carry arms. Perhaps this is why Peter Day was frightened, but if he thought that Garriock and Rossiter were night-hawks then he was mistaken. The night-hawks have some notable finds to their credit, including the Snettisham Bowl Hoard, the Icklingham Bronzes and the Wanborough Hoard; perhaps the finders of the 'Batheaston' hoard were night-hawks.

The dealer who buys from a dishonest vendor is putting himself and his colleagues at risk of handling stolen goods. The only way in which he can avoid this situation is by making detailed enquiries to ensure that the vendor has title. If need be he must interview the landowner and examine the agreement made with the metal detectorist. He must beware of provenances like 'Suffolk', 'Batheaston' and even 'recovered from a well in the Gloucestershire area'. Who can be trusted? Lord McAlpine learnt the hard way, but he really did learn. In an interview with the *Art Newspaper*, published in February 1998, he said that the problems over the Salisbury Hoard finally led him to give up as an antiquities dealer: "The risks of finding yourself in this kind of situation were high. It was a lesson, and a lesson that everyone is learning. I closed my business."

The rigorous research needed to establish title is more suited to archaeologists than dealers. Would it not be better to extend the Treasure Act to cover all antiquities? Objects of base metal, pottery and organics would then have the same protection as objects of gold and silver. All would belong to the Crown, and all would have to be reported. Of course there would be problems. There is no reliable estimate of the number of antiquities discovered in England each year, but it must run into thousands. A report by English Heritage and the Council for British Archaeology suggested that 400,000 antiquities dating before AD 1600 are now found each year, but that figure was calculated from inadequate data (though the only available data). Certainly the numbers are enormous, and there would have to be a big increase in the archaeological establishment in order to monitor them. There would be far too much work to involve coroners, but their role in Treasure Trove is an accident of history, and perhaps the time has come for it to pass into history. Instead, antiquities would have to be reported to a museum-based service, where qualified archaeologists would identify and record the antiquities. Those artefacts deemed sufficiently important to be retained by a museum would be valued, and those not required would be returned to the finder, as is the practice with artefacts covered by the Treasure Act. The finder would be offered a reward amounting to the full valuation of the artefacts retained, and if he disagreed with the valuation he would be able to appeal to an independent committee. In theory the landowner would lose out, because antiquities that would today belong to him would in future be the property of the Crown. But in practice there would be no problem, because the finder would have signed a 50:50 agreement with the landowner before any antiquities were discovered.

Such a system would be costly to run, in terms of staffing the archaeological service and purchasing finds for the museums. But if we really care about our antiquities these cost implications must be faced. We would be able to record, and if need be preserve, all our antiquities: England and Wales would come into line with most of the rest of Europe, and indeed with the rest of the United Kingdom because Scotland already has comparable legislation in place, and all antiquities found in Northern Ireland and the Isle of Man must be reported. We would be offering a fair deal to archaeologists, metal detectorists and landowners.

If all English antiquities were protected in this way dealers could easily check on the title to an artefact: its provenance and history would have been recorded by the archaeological service to which it was submitted. The open market in antiquities would certainly diminish, and dealers might have to seek other ways of earning a living: already Lord McAlpine has turned to other interests, and Sotheby's have now ended their regular Antiquities Sales in London. It may be argued that ending the open market will merely encourage the black market, but that is a risk that must be taken. There would be no black market if there were no collectors. Rich collectors with cabinets (and public exhibitions) of unprovenanced antiquities must be educated. But first the public and the politicians have to be educated: to be made aware of a tremendous loss that is masked because it is surrounded by secrecy and half-truths. The story of the Salisbury Hoard is important because it is extremely well documented. It exposes practices that no civilised country should tolerate. Something has to be done, and it has to be done quickly.

Index

air photographs 58–9, 60, 90
Allan, John 25
Anderson, Robert 6, 48, 54, 55, 85, 106
Anderson, Rose 6, 13, 39, 40, 41, 42–3
animals: bones 69, 70, 111, 112; figurines 120, 149, **Pl.18**
Antiquaries Journal 18
Antiquities Dealers Association 98
anvil 33, **Pl.6**
Armorican hoards 114
Arretine pottery 125–6
arrowhead 29, **Pl.16**
Art and Antiques Squad 6, 47, 48, 49
Art Newspaper 153
Arundel 25
Ashmolean Museum 6, 17, 18, 20, 104; Exhibition catalogue, McAlpine Collection 20, 21, 30, 32, 33, 39, 88
Atkins, Richard 6, 86, 89, 91, 92
Augustus 118
awls 122
axes, Salisbury Hoard 17, 27, 77, 78, 80, 106; flat 20, 22, 29, 30, 83, 113, **Pl.17**; flanged 29, 113, **Pl.17**; palstaves 27, 28, 110, 113, 120, **Pl.17**; socketed 22, 28, 30, 31, 110, 113; socketed, with 'high tin' content 28, 30, 43, 59, 67, 73, 75, 76, 79, 95, 97, 113-14, 123, **Pls.2, 3, 6, 17**;

joining pieces 81, 102, **Pl.15**; miniature 117; extraneous 76, 88, 104, **Pl.6**
axes, other sites 114, 119, 120, 122

Babcock 83
Bacon, Jo 142
Badman, John 77
Barker, Gordon 140
barrow 111
Basnett, Pete 6, 48, 54
Bath 39
'Batheaston' hoard 30, 39, 76, 117, 120-23, 152–3, **Fig.10**
Bavaria 131
Bawsey 135-7, **Pl.19**
Bemerton 22, 23, 31, 94; Farm 6, 38, 52, 53, 61, 69, 70
Bersu, Gerhard 111
Bimson, Mavis 131
Blofeld, Judge John 137
Blomeley, Ian 6, 58, 59, 60, 61, 64
Bognor Regis 24
Bohemia 128–9
Bonham's 41
Bournemouth 23
boxes 140–41, **Pl.21**
bracelets 128
Braham, Maurice 6, 17, 21, 36, 39, 76, 77, 81, 82, 88, 95–7, 104, 130
Bright 6, 65, 87, 90
Bristol 22
British Museum 6, 7, 8, 9, 11, 14,

16, 17, 22, 23, 29, 31–6, 39–42,
44, 53, 54, 57, 58, 60, 66, 75,
78, 80, 84, 86–9, 92, 93, 96,
97–8, 101–4, 107, 119–20, 129,
131, 133, 135–7, 141–7, 152;
Iron Age Gallery 101, 107;
Research Laboratory 131;
Society 141; Trustees 8, 11, 12,
16, 31, 57, 86, 88, 91, 102, 103
brooches 22, 28, 30, 53, 121,
122, 128–9, 134, 141–3, **Fig.11**;
unfinished 133
Brown, Stephen 137
buckles 28, 89
Burnett, Andrew 6, 42, 44, 45, 77,
79
Butser Ancient Farm 112

Cantabria 124
Canterbury: Archaeological Trust
141; Museum 141–4
Carter, Brian 18
cauldrons 117, 118, 128; miniature
17, 20, 26, 28, 30, 66, 75, 76,
86, 98, 115–18, 122, 123, **Fig.8**,
Pl.4; miniature, repaired 115
Cavill, Brian 6, 12, 23, 26, 33, 35,
36, 38, 39, 65, 73, 75, 76, 78,
82, 83, 88–90, 96, 98, 104, 109,
113
Council for British Archaeology
153; *CBA News* 75
chapes 28, 114, **Pls.5,6**
Charlbury 129–30
Checkland, Sarah Jane 81
Chilham Castle 141–4
chisels 27, 29, 30, 70, 78, 79, 110,
114, 119, 120, 122, **Pls.4,6,14**
Christie's 34, 43, 77, 78, 93, 103,
104, 129, 140–41
Cimbri 118
Cirencester Museum 17
Clayton, Peter 6, 12, 17, 31, 32,
33, 34, 35, 36, 38, 39, 40, 41,
43, 45, 49, 54, 55, 76, 82, 103,
142, 151
Clerkenwell Magistrates Court 85
Cockburn, Andy 6, 88, 94, 96
Coinex fair 26, 83, 95, 97
coins 52, 53, 78, 93, 120, 129, 130,

135, 140, 144–8, 151; hoards
80, 135, 145, 147–50
Conybeare, Clare 6, 11, 37, 38, 52,
54, 64, 70, 89, 97
Cook, Reginald 6, 52–4, 59–61,
65, 66, 69–71, 73, 75, 86, 87,
89, 90, 97, 98, 99, 101, 103,
106, 107, 151–2
Cornbury Park 129–30
Corney, Mark 6, 59, 60
coroners 134–6, 144, 146
Covent Garden market 18
Cowslip Farm 38
cremation burials 140-42
Croatia 127
crown 120
Crown Estates Commissioners 44
Crown Prosecution Service 80,
85–7
Crummy, Stephen 15, 19
Cumberland Hotel 36, 37, 93
Cummings, John 6, 22, 23, 25, 36,
37–40, 42, 54, 65, 66, 76, 77,
79, 80, 84, 85, 90, 92–9, 102,
104, 106, 109, 152
currency bar, miniature 83, 117
Cunliffe, Barry 112
Curtis, John 83

daggers 27, 29, 30, 35, 78, 110,
114, 120, **Pls.3, 6, 9**
Daily Mail 82, 90
Danebury 112, 119, 123
Daneswick 133, **Pl.20**
Davies Collection 129
Day, Peter 6, 12, 21–6, 31, 42, 73,
76, 80, 83, 84, 93, 94, 98, 106,
117, 153
Deal 114
Department of Culture, Media and
Sport 107, 151
Department of National Heritage
43, 106, 107
Devizes Museum 6, 17, 20, 22, 23,
25, 26, 32, 34, 77, 83, 84, 91,
93, 96, 98, 102, 135
dirks 114
discs 28
ditches 64, 111, 146–8
Dorchester, Dorset: hoard 17, 20,

22, 24, 25, 26, 37, 47, 94;
Museum 25
Dove, Simon 18
Drott 66,67,71,87, **Pl.11**
Dublin 41
Duchcov (Dux) 128–9
Dumez-Onof, Michel 129
Dunkels, Fran 6, 55, 75

Ede, James 77
Elsenham 140–42, 151, **Pl.21**
English Heritage 67, 71, 87, 153
Erskine, Robert 129, 132
Essendon 41, 66, 87, 144–5, 148
Essex Archaeological Unit 140
Evening Standard 81
Exeter Museum 25, 80
Exmouth 23, 25
export licences 78, 141, 143, 151

Farrer, Sir Matthew 58
Favenham 136
ferrules 22, 23, 73, 83, 117, **Pl.15**
Fincham 136
Fitzpatrick, Andrew 143
Fleischman, Lawrence 126
flints 67
Fowler, John 6, 23, 25, 77, 80, 101, 107
Foxton 71,133
France 104
Frankfurt 78
Franks, A.W. 119
funnels 28

game counters 140
Garriock, Jim ('John') 6, 7, 27–45, 47–55, 59, 65–7, 70, 71, 73, 75, 77, 82, 83, 85, 90–94, 96–9, 102, 104, 107, 109, 110, 151–3
Germany 78
Getty Museum 126
Gifford, Mrs 131
Glaisier, Dr 97
glass vessel 140
Glastonbury 77
Gloucestershire 14, 17, 26, 47;
Hoard ('Group 1') 21, 24, 25, 30, 32–3, 36, 40, 43, 44, 51, 55, 75, 88, 93, 101, 117, 153, **Pl.6**

Goldstein, Barbara 6, 78, 104
Goodwin 94
gouges 27, 29, 31, 78, 79, 82 ,99, 106, 110, 114, 122, **Pls.3,6**
grain storage 112
Grampian 117
Green, Barbara 21
Gregory, Tony 136–7
Griffiths, Nick 6, 37, 70, 83, 85, 86
Grover, Brian 104

Hadida, Susan 6, 98, 99
Hagbourn Hill Hoard 120, 122–3
hammers 28
Harris, Oliver 16
Hawkes, Christopher 119
Hay, Malcolm 6, 77–8, 84
Hayes, Justin 140
helmets 129–31, **Fig.12**
Hertfordshire Archaeological Trust 144
Hildyard Collection 14
Hodder, Charles 145–6
Holborn CID 6, 44, 49, 77, 89, 92, 96
Hordern, Judge Christopher 91, 96, 98–100
horn 70, 111
horn-cap 34, 35
horse-bits 120
Hounslow Hoard 119–20, 122, **Pl.18**
Hoxne Hoard 149
Hughes, Karen 12, 68, 116
Hungary 127
Hurly 90
huts 111–12

Iceni 135
Icklingham Bronzes 149–51, 153
India 125–6
ingots 114, 144, 148
Inheritance tax 103, 106, 107
Irish literature 118
iron slag 147–8
Isleham Hoard 118–19
Italy 125, 128

Japan 77

Jersey 78

Kelly, Eamonn 41
Keys, David 6, 23, 25, 26–9, 32, 34, 35, 39, 54, 55, 61, 64, 70, 75, 151
knife, with decorated blade 133, **Pl.20**
Knight, Jeremy 25
Knightsbridge Crown Court 87–9; trial 88–100; unused material (evidence) 85–7, 92

Laidler, Jonathan 6, 90, 91, 95, 96, 99
lamp, iron 140
La Tène 117
Lawson, Andrew 6, 20, 22, 24–6, 30, 33, 58, 75, 80, 93, 94, 151
Lebanon 127
Leintwardine 143
linch-pin 13, 14
Lincolnshire 79, 117
Limitation Act 102; Statute of Limitation 35
Littlehampton Museum 25
Little Woodbury 111
Liverpool 132; University 20, 137
Longworth, Ian 6, 11, 32–5, 44, 45, 47, 48, 51, 58, 70, 85, 103
Lowrie, Pam 6, 53, 59, 60, 69, 87, 90, 102, 103, 106, 107

McAlpine, Lord 6, 9, 13, 14, 16, 17, 20, 21, 23, 28, 31, 32, 36, 39–40, 43, 47, 55, 75, 77–9, 81, 82, 88, 90, 93, 95, 99, 101–4, 106, 107, 110, 123, 153–4
MacGregor, Arthur 20
McIntyre, Ian 18
magnetometer 59, 60, 62–4, 69, **Fig.3**
Mainz 131
Martin, C.J. 6, 20, 23, 25, 34, 37, 43, 54, 55, 76–9, 83, 95–6, 98
Martin, Sandy 129
Makey, Peter 6, 67, 69, 70
Marshall, Sandra 12
Massereene and Ferrard, Viscountess 141–4

Maurice 77
May, Jeffrey 79
Meridian TV 90
metal analysis 21, 137
metal detectors 33, 59, 65, 67, 69, 70
Miller, David 6, 17, 37, 42, 45, 55, 77, 95, 97, 131–2
Mills, Nigel 6, 18, 23, 37
mirrors 70, 141–4,
Moor, John 77
Morris, George 6, 35, 48, 85, 102
moustache objects 30, 33, 117–18, **Pl.16**
Munich 78, 131–2
Museums and Galleries Commission 106, 107
Mussel, John 6, 77, 95, 97

Narford 135
National Council for Metal Detecting 44, 133, 139, 151
National Heritage Memorial Fund 16, 102, 152
National Museums of Scotland 6, 31, 39, 76
Needham, Stuart 6, 11, 17, 33, 47, 49, 50, 51, 53, 54, 59, 60, 65, 69, 73, 80–83, 88, 89, 104, 106, 107, 122
Netherhampton 52, 59, 71; excavation 55, 57–71, 73, 76, 92, 110–11, **Fig.4**, **Pls.10-14**; compensation for excavation 66, 92; further excavation 75, 87, 90, 103–4; Hoard A = Salisbury Hoard; Hoard B 53, 63, 70, 71, 111, 123, **Pl.14**
Nether Wallop 114
Nichols, Darren 141–3
night-hawks 7, 69, 147–8, 152–3
Norfolk Archaeological Unit 136–7, 145–6
Northover, Peter 6, 21, 23, 31, 39, 76, 83, 137
Northampton, Earl of 127
Norwich: Castle Museum 21, 25, 104–6, 137; Crown Court 137

Oglethorpe 6, 89, 90, 103, 106